Dreaming of Eden

Reflections on Christianity and sexuality

D1471565

edited by Kathy Galloway

First published 1997

Wild Goose Publications
Unit 15, Six Harmony Row, Glasgow G51 3BA

Wild Goose Publications is the publishing division of the Iona Community.
Scottish Charity No. SC003794. Limited Company Reg. No. SCO96243.

ISBN 0947988 51 3

Cover: 'Dreaming of Eden' © 1997, Tiffany Lynch

Distributed in Australia and New Zealand by Willow Connection Pty
Ltd, Unit 7A, 3-9 Kenneth Road, Manly Vale NSW 2093.

Permission to reproduce any part of this work in Australia or New
Zealand should be sought from Willow Connection.

A catalogue record for this book is available from the British Library.

Printed by The Cromwell Press Ltd, Melksham, Wilts.

*... The land of innocence is not regained
when once it's lost, but on the farther coast
its joys, matured, redeemed, may be attained
even by those who count themselves as lost.
The flow of friendship, trust, this is the tide
that bears us safely to the other side.**

* Kathy Galloway, extract from 'Redeemed', *Talking To The Bones* (SPCK, 1996)

Contents

Introduction

Anyone who is bold enough, or rash enough, to enter the field of debate about Christianity and sexuality does so at their peril. Many of those who rushed or even tiptoed on to it are still nursing their wounds. Though people can and do challenge, contest and even change a whole range of Christian doctrine and teaching, from the Virgin Birth to the authority of Scripture; and though Christian practice has undergone many shifts this century on a range of social issues from labour relations to apartheid, from colonialism to disarmament, none of them has the capacity to generate quite the amount of passion as talking about sex. As one of the contributors to this book observes, 'the noisiest problem of all for Christians is sex.'

Of course, it's a subject close to most people's hearts, and it affects us very directly, in a way that other issues don't. But both in secular perceptions and in its own internal (and sometimes brutal) deliberations, the church talking about sex is also the church talking about power.

There has been a huge cultural shift from the power of the institutional to the power of the relational, which has not just affected the church, but many other institutions; government, the monarchy, law and order, education. No longer will people do things or agree things just because the police, teachers, or churches tell them to. Now they will ask questions, will reserve the right to disengage, and will be influenced as much by their relationship towards and within these bodies as by any tradition or dictat.

Because they like their own church, and the relationships within it, or because they love Jesus, or because they have a nostalgic affection for it, many people will go on giving the church their loyalty and commitment, while simply disregarding parts of its teaching they don't agree with. Sexuality is one huge area of church doctrine in which this is clearly the case. The traditional position on sexual intercourse is that it is not permissible in any circumstance except that of heterosexual monogamous lifelong marriage. But most Christians are not virgins when they marry. Many Christians divorce. Some Christians are practising homosexuals. Some live together outside marriage. And though there is still a consensus in secular as well as church circles that adultery is a bad thing, a betrayal of relationship, it is the deceit and faithlessness that is seen as the sin, not the actual sex. In the Catholic church, teaching on contraception is disregarded by the majority. In no other area of church life is the gap between theory and practice so wide.

There is a certain comfort in going on failing to address this fact. Some illusion of power can be maintained as long as it's not actually examined too closely. The scandals can be covered up, the errant clergy removed. The church can go on being theoretical, answering questions that no-one is asking. Meanwhile, the credibility gap grows — and the insights and testimony that Christians *do* have to offer in this relational world often go unheard. We are not interested in the testimony of the wounded. We prefer to campaign from the textbooks.

The maintaining of the façade of institutional power is a costly one. It can lead to dangerous falsehood; the one, for example, that says that children and young people should be protected from too much sex education, too much knowledge about sex, should be kept 'pure and innocent' lest they be drawn into premature sexual activity; when in fact, the unremitting evidence is that the more, and more accurate and earlier the knowledge, the *greater* the chance of young people avoiding teenage pregnancy and early sexualization, the greater their ability to be discerning and responsible in their choices.

For, after all, children and adolescents are growing up in a culture where learning about sexuality will not come primarily from the church, the school or, even, explicitly anyway, the home, but from *Neighbours* and *EastEnders* and *Brookside*, from the pages of tabloids and the newsagents' displays, from advertising and films, and, most of all, from the way adults behave. For some reason, we insist on acting as if children are stupid, as if they will not very clearly see through 'do as I say, not as I do'. And what, with acute powers of observation and assimilation, children see adults do, ranges across a huge spectrum of human behaviour, wherein criteria of love, respect and creativity in relationship and, conversely, those of hostility, abuse and stagnation cannot possibly be contained within one neat category, even in the church.

Like all of us, children learn from the actual, not the theoretical. Our children live in a society where, *de facto*, many of the old taboos have gone — against divorce, against premarital sex, against childbirth out of wedlock. Adults may lament the changing of the rules, may attribute every conceivable social and personal ill to their disappearance, may point to the suffering experienced, may be worried about what appears chaotic, even anarchic. Or adults may value the release of people from the prison of intolerable marriages, may believe that nothing good can come from what is imposed by fear or force of external pressure, may rejoice in the removal of punitive and pious stigmatization. Adults may think what they like. The fact remains that for children, the world they inhabit holds a wide variety of possibilities and choices, all, of course, with their consequences. In this world, the traditional stance of the church (which is primarily experienced as rules, not freedom) can seem not so much right or wrong as simply meaningless, non-sense, to do with some other world. And when one is perceived to be engaged with a theoretical, even imaginary world, rather than the real world, a large credibility gap opens up.

For another significant group of people in this society, the gap is where they fall. A recent and very large survey of sexual behaviour and attitudes discovered that the people most sexually active outside marriage (whether married or not) and likely to have the most sexual partners, were not young people but those in their thirties and forties. As people marry and have children later, as women enjoy a much greater degree of personal autonomy and financial independence than ever before, as social stigma against singleness wanes (it is estimated that by the end of the century, one-third of the population will live alone) and as permanence ceases to be the primary virtue in sexual relationships, with 'as long as we both shall *live*' being replaced with 'as long as we both shall *love*', a group is created which is independent of parental norms, and likely to engage in a wide variety of relationship styles.

But even more significant is the growing number of people in this age range who find themselves single anew as a result of marital breakdown. Since few marriages end without some degree of pain, this is a lot of hurt people. Struggling with feelings of anger, guilt, grief, fear, loss of confidence, trying to cope with hurt and confused children, financial worries, domestic upheaval, job insecurity, ambivalent friendships and often, the shattering of dreams and the questioning of previously secure belief systems, it is hardly surprising that adults who are anyway used to being sexually active should look to have needs which are not essentially sexual met sexually. Sex as anaesthetic, a way to numb the pain; sex as therapy or recreation; above all, sex as validation — 'I'm still an acceptable human being.' For those tiptoeing through this particular minefield, whose view of the church is frequently that it sees them as failures and treats them as an embarrassment, reiteration of the orthodox position can be hugely distressing, and add insult to injury.

And homosexual people may find themselves with questions about the nature of God which much of the church at present treats with contempt. Being told that we are made in the image of God is rather cold comfort if your particular embodiment of that is forbidden for the whole of your life to enjoy sexual delight with another person. What a comfortless, hopeless, brutal dogma. What father would give his son or daughter a stone when he asks for bread? Father God, it would seem, if his son or daughter is gay. And it is a narrow definition indeed of creativity that restricts generativity to making babies. An answer about sex is no use to someone asking a question about God.

What is the spirit?

George MacLeod, the Founder of the Iona Community, often said that if there was a spiritual question, you had to ask, what was the matter. But the reverse is also true. Perhaps the questions young people and wounded people and gay people are asking the church (if indeed, they are still interested in what the church has to say) are spiritual questions, expressing themselves in the language of sexuality, one of our most profound motivations. 'Where do I belong? Who am I? (or, who do *you* say that I am?) What am I worth? How can I care? Why does it matter?' These are existential questions that take on an added significance in times of transition, whether personal or social. And the tragedy for many now is that the collapse of what seems like a rule-based cultural conformity, too often imposed by the use and abuse of power, has left a void, because the church has ceased to be an explorer and has settled for the old, often inaccurate maps. Into this void, it is all too easy for the spirituality of the market, which is anything but free, to take root. You know the one. Everything can be bought, at a price, if you have the currency. Value is set by the market. Demand is highest for the glamorous, the undamaged, the rare, the curious. That which is damaged, imperfect, flawed, replaceable, isn't worth very much, can easily be dumped. There's no profit in containing needs, in limiting wants — just feed the appetite instead. And there are no limits to growth, never mind the environment (*that* can be policed).

In this spirituality, sex is a commodity to be bought and sold or to sell, though the currency may not always be the dollar or the Deutschmark. Or it is a hothouse flower, forced out of season, exotic, luxuriant, a spiritual mark of wealth — but not deeply rooted, unable to grow in harder soil when exposed to cold winds and climatic variations. And of course, it has in common with the older order the use of sex as control — of self, of others, of pleasure and delight, of justice and love.

We live in a time when the deepest and most painful need of the human person is for intrinsic worth, unconditional acceptance that does not depend on being good, right, controlled, conformist, *or* on being pretty, young, successful, rich, employed. Or on being straight, white and male. But if people do not hear the word that says, 'yes, you are accepted' through the meaningful framework of faith; if they do not hear it through their belonging within an accepting community; if they do not hear it through their closeness to the land; then people increasingly and only seek and hope to hear it in their personal, and especially sexual, relationships. This is too great a burden for any relationship to bear. Once again, worth becomes extrinsic, conditional, dependent. But the Word of life is unconditional, grace, a gift. Only those who have received this gift, who know themselves to be accepted intrinsically, unconditionally, can let go of the need to earn or pay for acceptance, and can be free to live responsively. That free gift is there for everyone. This is the testimony of those who follow Jesus. But both a law-based and a market-based sexual theology get in the way of the receiving of that gift, because they have no place in them for gratuity, for generosity, for the extravagant gesture.

Which is a great pity. Because what so often gets lost is authentic sexual liberation. We may have bondage but no discipline. We may have licence but no freedom. Artists know that there is no creativity without a system of formal constraints; parents know the truth of this. Lovers know the truth of this. Creativity of all kinds, in art, in prayer, in justice-making, in human relationships, is born where people wrestle with angels, outside Eden, on the border between heaven and earth, where they struggle to create a new form, a new song, a new template, a new ethic with all the discipline and passion they can bring to bear. Many of the old boundaries have shifted, and where they are now is risky, dangerous territory. We should expect to be wounded, as Jacob was.

What we should not expect, as church, is that people will pay any attention to us if we are not also struggling, to be found also lost on the uncharted ground, but are instead back in our own private Edens (which for many may actually be our place of exile — from ourselves, and from others, even, dare one say it, from God) issuing orders that are irrelevant to the real exploration.

It may be that in the struggle we will find once again that love is the fulfilment of the law. But we will have to discover that for ourselves, we are no longer content to take it on trust from those we no longer trust. Or it may be that the formal constraints are those of respect, trust, friendship, humour, delight in desire, pleasure in difference, celebration of unity. Our faith has much testimony worth listening to from those who have struggled on the outside, on the margins, even though it may have been in different contexts. What might it mean, for example, to apply the principles of non-violence, sacrificially worked out over centuries in the pursuit of the peaceable commonwealth, to our sexual relationships:

- respect for the partner, and for everyone involved as fellow human beings
- care for everyone involved in a relationship
- refusal to harm, damage or degrade people/living things/ the earth
- if suffering, loss is inevitable; willingness to take it on oneself rather than inflict it on others; not retaliating to violence with violence
- refusal to collude with injustice
- confronting the issue/s
- belief that everyone is capable of change
- recognition that no-one has a monopoly of the truth, so aims to bring together our 'truth' and the other's 'truth'
- belief that the means are the end in the making, so the means have to be consistent with the end
- openness rather than secrecy

And there are resonances with the mystical, contemplative strand of Christianity in the valuing of the affective, the intuitive and the bodily that characterizes much feminist and liberation theology today. It is practically the only place in Christian devotional literature in the West where sexual imagery and metaphor has been joyfully and unashamedly used.

But until we are courageous enough to engage with the deepest questions of the human spirit, our sexuality will remain crippled by burdens it was never meant to bear.

I find myself, as a Christian, unable to accept some of the traditional teachings of the church on sexuality. They are based largely on a consciousness I do not share, and do not wish to share. Obviously, I am not alone in this; large numbers of Christians do not adhere to them in practice and have no intention of doing so. And yet there are many ways in which my faith sustains and challenges and liberates me and others as sexual beings. The essays in this book do not set out to be a systematic alternative to traditional Christian doctrine, neither are they mostly an analysis of it. They are reflections from different vantage points, including the poems; reports from the gap, if you like. They are written by a diverse group of people whose age range spans more than half a century, who are Presbyterian, Episcopalian, Roman Catholic, Methodist, and who have written from their own experience.

One of the contributors, John Turner, an Anglican priest in Berlin, died during the writing of the book. Among his papers was found a few pages beginning his chapter. I wished to include it — though it is brief, it says a great deal. His friend and colleague, Peter Francis, till recently Provost of St Mary's Episcopal Cathedral in Glasgow, has finished the chapter, reflecting on John's own word made flesh. I have also included an essay John wrote for a short publication on the church's response to the HIV/AIDS virus.

I wish to thank the Iona Community for commissioning me to edit this book and the staff at Wild Goose Publications for their help.

I would especially like to thank the contributors to the book for their willingness to tackle the 'noisiest problem', and to be personal in doing so.

And I would like to pay my own tribute to John Turner, who was a friend, and whose loss to many is immense. He had the faith and courage, and the wit, to be himself, and he was loved for it.

> ... After all,
> this too is human,
> this too is true.
> If human is acceptably
> what I am, or you, or you,
> then I am this,
> and this is human,
> and there is no shame
> in being this.
> And this is, shameless, touching, who I am![1]

Muckraking

Precious things
are revealed
when the mud
subsides;
hidden things,
submerged
for years
(whether by accident or design),
will re-emerge
and realign
themselves
with the known world,
the outward
and the visible world.

This is cleansing
this healing
this revealing
this muckraking.

Insides and outsides: sexuality as life journey

One day, a long time ago, a four-year-old girl said to her mother, 'Mummy, I know the difference between men and ladies.' In her best understanding voice, her mother responded, 'Do you, dear? What is the difference?' The reply was as perceptive as it was succinct. 'Men have outsides and ladies have insides.'

Of course, if that was the only difference, then life might be a good deal less complicated. The truth is that we each have insides and outsides, and the whole journey of our lives is somehow to reconcile these parts not just in relation to our sexuality but to our self-esteem, personal identity, spirituality, all aspects of our lives.

What then is this sexuality — can it be defined? Definitions have ranged from the all-encompassing which seem to embrace the whole personality to the narrow focus of only sexual intercourse. Much of what we take for granted turns out to be speculation or prejudice. However, if we are to pursue our journey together, we have to attempt a shared understanding. I can only share some of my thoughts and experiences in the hope that some of my signposts may be helpful.

Recently there has been a great deal of controversy about sexuality especially in relation to gender identity and transsexuality, and many eminent people have made pronouncements — some of them concentrating on the significance of the inside, and some on the importance of the outside; our nature or our nurture. The sexual journey is both chronological, on a timescale from birth to death, and a constant movement from inside to outside and back. What is meant here by inside and outside?

Inside is not used, as the little girl used it, to mean the hidden female organs of reproduction, but represents the internal processes which are contained within ourselves; selves not solely as the physical bodies through which we interact with the world 'outside', but incorporating the minds and spirits which interpret and make sense of and initiate that interaction.

Outside represents all the external stimuli which act on us and which we then internalize and process before we respond or stimulate in our turn. My understanding of the journey, of its ages and stages, takes into account not only the maturing process which occurs internally over the years but also the messages which come to us from our environment, informing and modifying our feelings and behaviour. This needs to be emphasized because recent statements from both psychologists and theologians suggest that there is still strong pressure for people to opt for one or the other, nature *or* nurture, inside *or* outside, and this position is then used to make moral and ethical judgements in many areas of sexual practice.

In order to understand some of the influences, internal and external, it is necessary to remind ourselves of the scientific facts of sex and gender. Even before that, it is necessary to remind ourselves that science is not infallible, that science describes what it observes, produces theories and tests those theories in the light of present understanding. Some of these theories will turn out to be adequate to explain what is found, some will be provisional, some will need to be modified. Scientific 'fact' is just one signpost on our journey.

Inside me

The primary internal process, common to us all, is rooted in the individual cells of our bodies. The fact that, with a few specialized exceptions, the chromosomal and genetic make-up of each cell is both identical between our cells and unique to each individual is well-known — the X and Y chromosomes which define our cell gender are now part of our common understanding — but we do need to remind ourselves that it is only in the second half of the twentieth century that this was described and explained. Sometimes I think we forget just how recently even the most basic description of the genetic contribution to sexuality took place. For centuries, including most of the Christian era, it was believed that the seed of human life was planted whole and entire by the male and that the female role was to provide the environment, the nest, in which the foetus could develop until able to live independently. Thus the mother made no direct contribution to the genetic make-up of her child, all its basic characteristics must be from the father. Seminal fluid carried fully equipped seeds of life needing only careful nurture to become human beings. If we look at some of the sexual taboos of the past, including attitudes to male masturbation, they become more logical in the light of this belief.

This journey has started with biological signposts, pointing to one of the pathways of understanding. As far as we know now, excluding cloning, we as persons start life as two cells, two half-people, a sperm cell contributed by the male parent and an ovum contributed by the female. Each of these cells contains half of the genetic material necessary to define one unique individual, and it is in their fusion that the potential person becomes a reality, one individual person with male or female characteristics, a little 23XY boy or a little 23XX girl, or, less commonly, another variation where the chromosomes have behaved differently.

Even at the cellular level, it is not just as simple as that. We may have described scientifically the chromosomal make-up of the cells, but we still have to explain how this leads to the characteristics which distinguish Jack from Jill, or even Jack from John. The genes on these chromosomes must in some way be able to control the development of the organs of the body so that the potential expressed in the original cell make-up becomes the reality of the human being. The amount of scientific research in this area at present is immense. The mapping of the human genome, that is, of all the genes which go to defining our species, is well under way, and yet we may not be much further forward in our philosophical understanding of what it is to be human. The mechanics are there, but the poetry is still missing.

The embryo is now defined cellularly as male or female but that particular X or Y chromosome still has to exert its influence on the development and differentiation of the body of the foetus so that when the baby is born the midwife can say with confidence, 'It's a girl' or 'It's a boy.' The gene has to 'express' itself. In fact, a lot of the research in this area is done on rats rather than humans, so our understanding of this stage is less than complete, and is often known more by the times when it goes wrong than by 'normal' development. It is known that the genes control whether the sex organs which develop are testes or ovaries, and these then define further development. The way this is done seems to be through the production of minute amounts of chemicals, sex hormone, at a crucial stage in embryonic development. Even here there is ambivalence, as these chemicals are very closely related, and a slight 'mistake' in the genetic message may change the structure of the hormone and the ultimate outcome of the process. In these rare situations, a chromosomally female foetus may develop male characteristics or vice versa.

The testes or the ovaries as the basic sex organs then control through the secretions of other chemicals the secondary characteristics which make us recognizably male or female, penis and scrotum, or clitoris, vulva and vagina. So there is even less confusion for the midwife. Most of us are born with the anatomical configuration to match our cellular structure. Most, but not all, have the appropriate hormone secretions to sustain this sexual development throughout life. If life was simply mechanical then there could and would be no confusion about sexual identity, but we know that the expression of genetic characteristics is not an all-or-nothing affair. If it were, we could not have the infinite variety of hair colour, skin colour, height, intelligence and all the other personal characteristics which are known to be genetically determined. Modern scientific thought is that the expression of a genetic characteristic is a spectrum of possibilities. Using only our simple powers of observation, this would seem to make sense and supports the conclusion that femaleness and maleness are not exclusive, but co-exist in balance in each individual.

This, of course, also makes it easier to understand the situation of people who feel ambivalent about their gender or even know themselves to be wrongly classified anatomically from an early age. It helps us to accept those whose physical sex is already at odds with their chromosomal or hormonal gender and those whose make-up differentiates them from the majority of the population. In the past, in Western society at least, these individuals often ended up in the alternative worlds of the circus, the brothel or the anatomy museum. Even in our enlightened, liberal society today, there may be precious little acceptance for them. Is it possible that by accepting our own mixed sexual nature, male *and* female, not male *or* female, we might be able to extend our understanding to others? Is it possible that it is our awareness of our own ambivalence which so frightens us that we cannot comfortably accept it in others?

At the moment of birth, potential becomes actual, our bodies are now entirely our own, separated from our mother and no longer able to rely on her hormones and metabolism. We are ourselves, solitary and unique, with all the genetic potential we will ever have. The drama is ready to unfold and within the drama, the foundation of the strand of sexuality is already laid.

Outside in

In these first days and weeks we are bombarded with sensations as we first experience the outside world; our eyes, our ears, our noses, our mouths, our skin, our muscles, our lungs, our gut, every sensory nerve-ending is stimulated and every impulse needs to be made sense of. In these first few months we are learning to feel, to be sensual, and in doing this we are deeply influenced by the environment around us. These external influences will, from the first moment, add to our understanding of who we are and of what we are doing here — the basic questions of existence which underlie not just psychology but also spirituality and religion.

The infant, you or me, is born as a bundle of sensations with the ability to think and feel and act appropriately to her perception of those sensations — but with a very limited understanding. The baby has little real power over her environment, only the power which she can exercise in an instinctive way by touching raw nerves in those around her ... guilt or hurt or love. She has no experience to tell her whether an event is significant or not, whether it is a frequent happening or a one-off, whether it represents a universal truth or an individual distortion. She has no source of information to explain her responses, no language to understand them. She has few choices within her control, not even the mobility to embrace or withdraw from sensations. Experiences at this stage are absorbed uncritically, unfiltered by judgement or experience, without knowing what is appropriate or inappropriate, acceptable or not to be accepted.

Later, as we begin to recognize sensations, we become aware of needs within ourselves. We feel an unpleasant gnawing in the pit of the stomach, we discover that this feeling is altered to a pleasant feeling of wellbeing when we are fed; we recognize the need for food-hunger. We feel solitary and fearful, we discover that the sense of security returns when a caring person attends to us, we recognize the need for relationship. We learn to feel and later to put a name to the feeling. If at this stage we are treated with indifference or inconsistency our emotional development is delayed or distorted, and with it our early sexuality.

It all sounds pretty straightforward, but things are never quite what they seem. In all our learning and growing we are not in a vacuum, we are surrounded by other people — with their own understanding, their own prejudices, their own agendas. Everything we learn will be influenced by them, by the messages they pass on to us. This is not a new idea; even in Old Testament times the handing down of negative influences had been observed: 'I will not fail to punish children and grandchildren to the third and fourth generation for the sins of their parents.' *(Numbers 14:18)*

Latterly it has been of particular interest to psychologists who are concerned with child development and family therapy, and can be studied in the works of Eric Berne, Virginia Satir and R. D. Laing. Our response to sexual feelings throughout our lives will be coloured by the messages we were given.

So, following conception and chromosomal sex and anatomical sexual identity at birth we learned to feel, to recognize feelings and to name feelings. These feelings include early sexual feelings, the comfort of a cuddle or a pat, the joy of a warm damp nappy, the sweet, soft feel of the nipple. And through the messages we received, we also learned to deny feelings or wrongly attribute feelings; for example, the temper tantrum to which the response is, 'You're just tired, dear.' Am I tired or am I angry and how am I to know? And if we are offended by the possibility of infants with sexual feelings, can we be sure we are not responding to the negative messages we were given?

Inside out?

In discovering feelings, we will inevitably have experienced the dark side of ourselves, the feelings which could be destructive to ourselves or others, the sibling jealousy, the wish to destroy or eliminate rivals, the cruel and sadistic impulses which are present in all of us. One of our tasks on this journey will be to learn how to deal with these. Sadly, our culture often prohibits any open discussion of these feelings with children.

It is, of course, thanks to Freud that we can now recognize the significance of our ability to accept or repress this 'dark side' and one factor in this is whether or not we are allowed to acknowledge these negative feelings, we now know that unacknowledged feelings, denied or distorted, lie at the root of much misery and personal damage.

Some milestones

Throughout our childhood, with all the other things we are learning, we are learning more about feelings and more about relationships. Firstly relationships with our primary carers, later with a wider range of people. The foundations of our adult sexuality are being laid and our beliefs about who we are and how we relate to others are being refined.

While overtly sexual behaviour by children is not normally encouraged, we have to acknowledge that there are times and places where sexiness in children is not discouraged, and more extremely, situations where children are indeed used as objects of sexual gratification, usually for adults. Freud found this difficult to accept, and attributed what we would now accept as evidence of child sexual abuse to the fantasies of hysterical women!

As far as we are permitted to develop our sexuality appropriately, the next milestone comes at puberty, when the physical changes in our bodies accelerate, our hormones proliferate and our gender and sexuality become linked to the possibility of procreation — the whole new possibility of pregnancy. Sexual feelings become more than just a pleasant glow, and may seem frightening in their intensity. We experience change in our bodies, in our emotions and in our social status and expectations. We have to contend with fluctuating physical sensations, with menstruation or erections; the physical indicators of gender and sex cannot be ignored, at least by ourselves. We are male and female for the world to see — anatomically at least.

We are also increasingly aware that we are expected to direct our sexual feelings to some specific objects (or subjects). This is generally assumed to be a physically attractive member of the opposite sex. This is the message aimed at us by our family and friends, but very few of us are going to be as clear-cut as all that. For many of us, our interests will swing about with our hormones. Most adolescents feel sexual attraction to members of the same sex as well as the other sex, but this is not comfortably acknowledged. Some will become mainly orientated in one or other direction, some will remain bisexual. The whole spectrum of responses is available.

In some societies puberty is the signal for the beginning of breeding; in our culture this is usually delayed. This brings us to a new milestone — the separation of conception from the physical act of sexual intercourse. In the past, the only way to avoid pregnancy with any certainty was to avoid intercourse, and for that, many tactics were employed. One was to keep young people, especially girls, ignorant about the mechanics of intercourse, and thus supposedly uninterested. This was often combined with dire hints about the brutal nature of the opposite sex — or of the conniving and predatory nature of the opposite sex — depending on your viewpoint. The church was able to go further by indicating the likelihood of burning in the fires of hell if one indulged in premarital frolics! The efficacy of such tactics can be found in the literature of past centuries, Robert Burns being a useful starting point. The damage of such tactics can also be found in literature and in the writings of the early psychoanalysts.

Today our sexuality can be unhooked from its consequences of breeding (not the only significant consequence, but the one emphasized by the church over past years) and indeed, the links between conception and sexuality have become tenuous as well. Embryos can be created mechanically, an act of masturbation being the nearest their creation will come to sexual arousal. In animals, if not yet in humans, embryos can be cloned, thus dispensing with any sexual activity at all.

More and more, the expression of our sexuality has to be related to personal gratification and mutual satisfaction of needs. This is still a new landscape to be explored, and the signposts are few and far between. There has been so much emphasis in the past on the relationship in adult life between sexuality and procreation, breeding, that it can be difficult to look at a broader picture.

Sexuality in adult life is the mature development of all that has gone before. It encompasses the powerful sexual attraction which culminates in orgasm, the warm sensual pleasure of touch and stroking, the desperate need for release from pent-up emotion, the single-minded channelling of all inner energy into one creative purpose. In all of these it carries both an awareness of the inclusiveness of humanity and yet our personal individuality; the search for integration which demands response to others to stimulate our awareness of ourselves — as creators. Maybe this is what sexuality is really about; creation, not just procreation; relatedness and sensual pleasure and self-expression and creativity. If we ourselves are created as sexual beings, then how can we fail to express our sexuality in all we do.

What is sex for?

In reality, sexual expression is found in all societies in all ages. In the sacred scriptures of all the major religions it is described, though in some more positively than in others. In the visual arts sexual symbolism has always been present, in literature erotic imagery is frequent. Yet, even as we accept that, many of us feel a check on our enthusiasm. Expressing ourselves as sexual beings feels dangerous and ill-disciplined. We are aware of the strict and rigid boundaries which have been set up to ... to do what? To protect us from our base, carnal natures? To protect us from unwanted pregnancy? Truly both of these, the internal and external threats.

Externally the control of creativity is the protection of power structures. In order to ensure that the child is indeed from the seed of the father, the woman must have no access to other men. To protect the inheritance of family wealth or status there can be no dispute about paternity. Women are weak intuitive creatures controlled by wandering wombs (hysteria) or premenstrual tension, and society must be protected from their irrational behaviour. Now that the myth of hysteria has been destroyed and it is accepted that men have hormonal cycles as well; now that extra-marital couplings do not need to result in pregnancy and DNA-testing can confirm paternity, perhaps the major external pressure is the fear of sexually transmitted disease, a real fear, but surely not God purposefully denying pleasure?

But even when the need for external controls is diminished, most of us still feel constrained. There is still fear, inside, but of what? Fear of the unknown, the worst kind. Fear of the strong feelings we knew but were not allowed to acknowledge in the past, the feelings which, when ignored, did not go away but attached themselves to other situations, claimed other names and are now expressed in other ways — in aggression, in manipulative passivity, in addiction, in self-destructive behaviour. The fear seems appropriate. I am not saying that all social pathology is the result of repressed sexuality, life is much more complicated than that, but I am saying that there is adequate evidence that it causes confusion and misery in ourselves and in our communities, and we need to ask what Jesus has to say about this, what is the gospel response?

I write this in the only way I can, as myself, female, conceived, born and raised in Scotland, with all that that means in terms of cultural, religious and educational influences.

I expect that as a child I must have had some awareness of sexuality but I did not have the language to express this. In some ways this is still a problem. The words we use in sexual expression tend either to be clinical and sterile or to have been prohibited to nice girls like me. Certain words were not to be repeated ... indeed, were not to be acknowledged as having been heard. The words in themselves did not seem to mean anything, but were 'dirty'. Lots of things were 'dirty' — such as dog dirt (never use the word 'shit'), human excrement and urine, food that had been on the floor or been sucked by another person, and the 'private parts'. In general it was best to avoid all mention of things dirty to avoid conflict or embarrassment. Thus questions were not asked and there was a lot of confusion in my mind.

Going to church and Sunday School was, by contrast, a very 'clean' activity. It involved clean face and hands and knees, clean socks and polished shoes, brushed hair, a clean hanky and going to the toilet before you left home. Purity was the badge of the Christian child and so is it any wonder that bodily functions and the Christian story never formed any positive connections in our lives. Body and spirit were separate and antagonistic, although we may have been left with a vague suspicion that there might be a further mystery to be initiated into as adults.

The clue, the signpost to this mystery, was to be found in the Bible no less. Because as our reading skills progressed, we discovered or were initiated into the 'dirty' bits in the Bible. Some of the words on the banned list were there, like womb and intercourse and pregnant, and in the Law of Moses we found activities described that we had never in our wildest dreams imagined. But, of course, these bits were never mentioned in Sunday School, and we never dared to ask.

Mapping the way ahead

How are Christians, how is the church going to respond to the new landscape? At present it seems that in fear of losing the way we try still to travel the old road. We have not yet found a safe path through the new territory. Parents and ministers and teachers fearful of the unknown set up signposts; 'here be dragons', like the maps of old.

We have followed many different paths on this journey so far, a journey for which we were given no map, or perhaps it was just that our map had been drawn by others with even less knowledge than ourselves. Some ways have turned out to be dead-ends, some have been fruitful diversions, some led to important viewpoints and others to the darkest depths. At times we were on solid ground, at times thought we were lost for good. As we explore the new territory, maybe the most we can do is to try to leave a few signposts for those who might follow.

In life there are experiences over which we have ultimately little control; birth, death and orgasm. It is in these moments above all that, consciously or not, we recognize the utter interrelatedness of our physicality, our sexuality and our spirituality; our embodiment and our 'out-of-bodiment'. If our Christian belief is of Incarnation, of embodiment, then it is necessary to take bodies seriously and necessary to consider the place sexuality has in the divine order.

Faith mother

I feel your nearness more acutely now
old woman: the last to be freed
from cruel joke and mocking cliché.

No longer put to death as witch
but often confined as confused
Your seeing is threatening,

(at menopause they say
women often see the devil)

and stands in the way
of conformity to a pattern
in which the human body is beautiful
only if it is young, shapely
and smells good.

But like Sarah long ago
you can still laugh
at the overlarge egos
of old men
hungry for lost dreams.

Your inner beauty
is the mysterious wisdom
of a heart, as yet, unbowed.
Your long and earthy memory
contains the experience of ages
of seeing and being
of waiting and pondering
all things in your heart.

Your ancient understanding
could even now be our hope
and our salvation.

Biblical insights and deforming practices

A tribe became convinced that God was present in all the ups and downs of their history, teaching them how to live. The knowledge they gained was not just for themselves. It was instructive for the way in which all humanity should manage life. People with prophetic insight recorded the tribe's experiences. These included insights for dealing with sexuality and sexual relationships.

But the result, set out in the books of the Bible, is no straightforward 'reading-out' of God's will and way. There are deep insights, but the reader has to win these in a struggle for light. A great variety of responses to God's presence are recorded: that brings with it a need to sort out what is genuinely 'of God', what only appears to be so, and what runs contrary to God's purposes. A variety of historical and cultural contexts are covered; in these, we have to sort is what is of lasting significance. Account must also be taken of a great variety of ways of communicating — straight narrative, parable, drama, poetry and other forms. On matters of sexuality, those who seek light in the Bible have to use their imagination, cultivate gifts of discernment, and invest energy and thought to get perceptions of God's will and way for human living out of all the varied evidence the Bible presents.

For Christians, the focus for doing so will be on Jesus Christ himself. That perspective is given in the opening words of the letter to the Hebrews: 'In the past God spoke at many times and in various ways to our forefathers through the prophets; but in these last days has spoken to us by his Son.' We engage in a search to discover what comes through, both from the earlier writings and from that life.

Over the centuries, dominating viewpoints have conscripted biblical texts which seem favourable to their positions. The Bible itself provides alternative texts which can challenge such selections. An examination of approaches which have had a dominating influence in society can be illuminating.

1. Patriarchy

The assumption underlying patriarchal attitudes is that men were meant to be in charge in life while women were destined to accept accessory roles, mainly those of providing men with heirs and looking after the home. This way of looking at life has often been so strongly embedded in the mentality of societies in which men monopolized power positions that it was considered to be unchallengeable. If it were to be challenged, defenders of patriarchal positions might have recourse to the Book of Genesis. There, insights of the Hebrew people, gleaned through many centuries of experience, are brilliantly set out in story form. They deal with the relationship between God and human beings, between human beings and one another, and between both and the natural order. The account given in the first chapter concentrates on the place of human beings in relation to God and to the rest of creation. The account given in chapters two and three adds insights on the relationship of male and female.

Defenders of patriarchy might argue for their position from these passages, pointing out that:

- the male was created before the female;
- the female was the one who gave in to temptation;
- the male takes a dominating role to which the female submits;

What alternative evidence could be quoted?

In chapter one of Genesis, women and men are treated as a partnership and are put in charge of creation together, as God's trustees. Neither is depicted as superior to the other. This emphasis continues in chapter two. The rib of the man, the basis on which the woman is *'built'*, suggests a side-by-side relationship. The declaration that together they make 'one flesh'— that is, one total humanity, each complementing the other — confirms the picture of a life of equal sharing.

If it were argued, from these accounts, that one sex had a higher rating than the other, the palm must surely be accorded to the woman. She is the crown of the whole creative process. She is made of human stuff, while the man is made of earth stuff, activated by God's inbreathing. It is the man who leaves father and mother to cleave to her so that they become 'one flesh'; not the other way round. The tempter recognizes her to be a tough opponent whom he must make sure he masters; and she shows her mettle by correcting his account of God's command. In contrast to her, the man is a weak 'fall-guy'. But the emphasis on a partnership of equals stands as the definitive emphasis.

Where the male is depicted as dominating the submissive female in chapter three, that situation appertains to an order of life spoiled by sin, one which cries out for remedy. It is not a way of living to be adopted but to be repudiated.

So in these profoundly illuminating stories there is an early pointer to the New Testament conclusion: 'There is neither ... male nor female [in status], for you are all one in Christ Jesus.'

'They have stolen our names,' cried Katherina Halkes, Dutch theologian, to my wife, Margaret, and myself, reflecting her outrage at the way in which women's decisive role in biblical history had been overlooked or ignored. In that history, the patriarchs play a decisive part. But the significance of that part is dependent on a promised line. Not any offspring could bear the promise; and the men had to wait for late and difficult births — it was as if God were reminding them of their dependency for the fulfilment of that promise on their wives. The account of the Exodus does not start with Moses and the burning bush. Before that, there was an all-woman exercise comprising midwives, a mother and sister, a princess and her train, without which there would be no Moses. It was a woman with ointment who provided dramatic testimony to the significance of Jesus Christ's death; and Mary Magdalene and other women who were witnesses to the resurrection (in a society in which a woman's testimony had no validity in a court of law!).

Patriarchy has no theological foundation to justify it.

As much as anything, inclusive language has undermined its influence. Every advance to equal partnership in church and state undermines it further. The church over centuries imbibed patriarchal assumptions. It is all the more guilty in that it had biblical resources to hand to criticize these and to affirm the equal partnership of women and men in God's sight.

2. Abstract principles

To approach questions of human sexuality from the vantage point of abstract principles is to make assumptions based on the primacy of thought, status and power. It is to start at a point several removes from reality:

- Thought is given priority over life-experience as if it provided a higher source of insight to draw on. Liberation theology insists that it forms the second not the first step in understanding how to live;

- A position of pre-eminence is given to the abstract thinker, who may be remote from, and ignorant of the stuff of life;

- Power is ascribed to many who are ill-equipped to handle it. Celibate male clergy are sexual beings and have their contribution to make. But if they take on themselves to legislate on matters of sexual conduct, that represents an attempt not to enlighten but to control the behaviour of others from a vantage point of inexperience.

Burdens are laid on people's shoulders. To start in the abstract and move in a gingerly way towards the real requires a thick texture of rules, regulations, interpretations and judgements to cover the great array of concrete circumstances which do not fit easily into theoretical categories. Jesus said of the scribes and Pharisees, preoccupied with such minutiae: 'They make up heavy loads and pile them on the shoulders of others, but will not themselves lift a finger to ease the burden' *(Matthew 23:4)*; One contemporary instance can be given: it takes minds extravagantly remote from reality to decree that contraceptive devices interfere with the loving congress of partners. Do false teeth interfere with their loving conversation?

People who struggle to handle sexual power in a responsible manner, who may be striving to act as responsible parents, have been disabled by arguments developed from abstract principles and thus refused the 'life abundant' which Jesus Christ came to bring. His coming in a body removed the legitimacy of such approaches.

3. Purity and contamination

In the Old Testament, the *Torah* ('Teaching', 'Law', 'Guidelines for living') distinguished categories of cleanness and uncleanness. These applied not only to animals but to human beings. Women particularly suffered. Times of menstruation were treated as times of uncleanness. Childbirth had to be followed by the observance of a time of purification (significantly, this was twice as long for a girl as for a boy). Sexuality itself is sometimes spoken of in the Bible as if it had a dubious rating (whereas that rating really applied to incest, adultery and intercourse within the prohibited degrees).

It is a power which proves hard to handle. Bodily urges and bodily rhythms were only too easily fastened on as particular sources of evil.

But this contradicts the fundamental biblical insight that we are all-of-a-piece, body-soul beings (in Scots we can say, 'look at that body over there — isn't she a poor old soul?'); and that, as a *totality*, we are in the image of God. We are not a mixture of pure 'spirit' and impure 'flesh'. Our sexuality is part of our whole being; and plays its part in all relationships.

When I was in Selly Oak Colleges, I was asked by the social studies lecturer to take a class for two sessions on sexuality. He warned me that if I failed to get their attention right from the start, I would lose them. So I began: 'I have a sexual relationship with my secretary, and she is a married woman.' They were all ears! They continued to give full attention, even when I went on to point out that the idea of sexual relationships is inaccurately limited in people's thoughts to sexual intercourse. Our sexual ways, feelings, angles on life can enrich every partnership (including that of dean and secretary).

The idea that the sexual part of our nature can be a contaminating part has had influence in the Christian tradition particularly because of the stated position of Augustine of Hippo. He identified human sexuality as a conduit for the transmission of original sin from generation to generation. He considered virginity to be superior to the married state. For him, the flesh lusts against the spirit. But his position was based on Stoic and Platonic thinking. It contradicts the fundamental biblical insight that we are a body/soul unity. Still it did much damage.

Throughout history, human thought and conduct has been plagued by an artificial division of flesh and spirit. In the Bible the Greek word for flesh, 'sarx', covers a great range of meanings. It can refer simply to our human state: 'all flesh is grass' *(Isaiah 40:6)*. It can refer to that human state corrupted: 'sins of the flesh'. What is illegitimate is to relate the word particularly to our sexual nature. The reference is to our whole nature. 'Sins of the flesh' listed in Galatians 5:19 (see also Romans 1:29, 30; 8:5-13) fall into four categories:

- sexual: fornication, unrestrained appetites, sexual irresponsibility;
- religious: idolatry and witchcraft;
- personal and social: feuding, wrangling, jealousy, bad temper; quarrels, divisions, factions, enviousness;
- excess: drunkenness, orgies.

Those who put Robert Burns and a pregnant lass on stools of repentance to face a congregation's judgement were clearly unaware that their vindictiveness was as much a sin of the flesh as illicit intercourse.

4. Sensual gratification and knowledge

Partly as a reaction to the horrors of the First World War and its consequences, the 1920s saw a sexual explosion marked by jazz, short skirts, the Charleston and other dances which encouraged spontaneity and uninhibited invention; and brought a sense of sexual liberation. A major difference between that and the 'swinging 60s' was the arrival of 'the pill', a reliable contraceptive. People were faced, seemingly, with opportunities for sexual intercourse without consequences, for the first time in human history. There was genuine liberation in this development. Parents could make responsible choices about the size of their families. Some who were caged in marriages which had died could break clear without having to face social condemnation (Orthodox churches can, in a measure, interpret 'till death us do part' so as to include the death of the marriage). As the century progressed, violence against women and abuse of children were brought out into the open where they could be dealt with. Partnerships in which work, home and childrearing duties were shared became more common. Matters of sexual conduct were debated more openly, knowledgeably and honestly.

But with these gains came a good deal of superficiality in sexual relationships. A strengthening of feminism challenged this trend. It was as if women enjoyed a fling, and then paused. Were they becoming merely an improved version of blow-up dolls, offering receptacles to accommodate straining penises: usable and discardable objects? It was time to affirm their dignity and significance.

For such a perception, the biblical understanding of sexual intercourse is relevant. It is a form of knowing! The Hebrew word 'yada' serves equally to describe entering another person sexually and getting to know God. Sexual intercourse is designed to allow two loving persons to get deeper into one another's beings, to search one another out, to take responsibility for one another, to deepen their commitment to one another. It is not just bodies which are penetrated. It is persons. In that lies the horror of rape, the uninvited intrusion into the core of another being's life. If it is deprived of that element of 'knowing', of sussing one another out, sexual congress can be a damaging experience.

The Jesus revolution

By his attitude and actions, Jesus released people into a fuller life and restored partnership which had been damaged.

1. He treated women in a way which flouted contemporary conventions. They were in the company of his disciples. He was willing to be instructed by a Syro-Phoenician woman; to relate to a Samaritan woman so that she became a missionary; to be prepared for death and burial by a woman and her ointment; to make women first witnesses to the Resurrection. In the last week of his life, he confronted the patriarchal powers of secular and religious establishments, and, crushed by them, reduced their pretensions to tatters.

2. He treated the *Torah* as an assembly of 'direction-finders.' He was prepared to indicate where its regulations were marked not only by divine sanction but also by the hardness of men's hearts; and affirmed that the provisions existed to serve human need, not to contain and crush it (Mark 2:23-28). To use another picture, he related to the Law as a vet would relate to an animal whose time has come, drawing out the kicking life within, enabling new birth.

In face of regulation-oriented religion, Jesus' attitude was permissive. He was, after all, the Son of an incredibly permissive Father. In the parable of the Prodigal Son, God is depicted as a householder who sells up half his estate and entrusts it to a hotheaded young man who proceeds to squander it. God will go to great lengths to enable us to learn from experience! It must be of our own will that we take his way. In the parable of the vine-dressers, God flies in the face of all the available evidence in saying: 'they will reverence my son.' The consequences of the sending had to be faced. Jesus did not decide for people how they should behave. He left them to work that out. Only by doing so could they become mature human beings growing into the fullness of life which God had prepared for them. They had the Law and the Prophets to guide them. More significantly, they had his own life. So he pushed back on challengers and questioners the need for responsible thinking and action on their part. People might look to him for pat answers. He would return the ball to their own court, freeing them to work out responsible decisions for themselves.

His actions made this clear.

- Faced with the contrived set-piece of the woman taken in adultery (if it was 'in the very act', where was the man?) he faced the accusers with the need for self-examination. It was their own judgement on themselves which made them withdraw.

- Asked to give a ruling on divorce, he was prepared to condemn the one-sided divorce of his day which deferred to male power-positions: but then he pushed back on his questioners the need to struggle with the meaning of being 'one flesh', a description of committed sexual relationships.

- 'render to Caesar what is Caesar's and to God what is God's', *(Matthew 22:21)* indicated the need for a continual search for light on how political authority related to God's authority.

His teaching made this clear.

- The most learned were no better placed than the illiterate to get to the heart of his parables. That form of teaching permitted people from all sorts of backgrounds to perceive some truth and work out what it meant for their own lives, or to reject the implications for themselves. Only so could they grow up. (Ephesians 4:11-16)

3. Jesus reminded his hearers that external ritual washings may do nothing to cleanse the mind and spirit (Mark 7:1-8). His own incarnation was a sign that holiness lies not in being set apart *from* the world but being set apart *for* God *in* the world.

To be pure, you need to do whatever the demands of the Kingdom of God require, however dirty your hands get in the process and however badly your reputation suffers (Philippians 2:6, 7, Matthew 5:11, 12). Real contamination comes from withdrawal from life's demands into some safe haven. It also stems from setting your heart on getting wealth and status, and getting your own way with others, sexually and otherwise.

As for physical contamination, Jesus simply broke taboos. He sought the company of social undesirables. He was with the poor, who were designated sinners since it was impossible for them both to observe the fine points of the Law and get enough to survive on for one day at a time. He touched the diseased to heal them. According to the Law, any man suffering from physical infirmity was impure and could not become a priest — Jesus treated infirmities not negatively as if they were punishment for past sins but as an opportunity for showing forth God's glory (John 9:1-7).

A church which separates itself off from seamier aspects of life and seamier kinds of company cannot be his church. A church which keeps its hands clean from sexual and other controversy cannot be his church. But pagan ideas of purity invade faith. In our time, the idea that the church should steer clear of political commitments is one such invasion. It would make of Jesus Christ a household god, concerned with personal and domestic affairs but not with how the world is run.

4. Jesus affirmed that all that the Father had made known to him, he had shared with his disciples. This knowledge included not only information but all that developed in a committed relationship — God and human beings getting into one another's minds and hearts. We can take our cue for our own sexual conduct from the nature of that fundamental relationship. In sexual intercourse, are we looking for gratification and emotional satisfaction? There is good not harm in that — if the relationship is sensitively and thoughtfully deepened thereby, by partners who love and respect one another. Where there is harm is where the 'knowing' factor is missed out by those bent on extracting for their own pleasure part of what another person has to offer while rejecting and discarding unwanted parts.

The priestly people

At different points of history, faced by different terms for living, operating under different pressures, human beings are called to work out responsible sexual relationships. What resources can they draw upon?

There is the Bible and the struggle, shared with others, to get to the heart of its insights.

There is the Holy Spirit illuminating human minds so that genuine direction-finders can be identified and all that Jesus Christ's life meant can be brought to bear in the lives of those who want to live truly today.

There are the priestly people.

Churches adhere to the belief that the decisive priesthood or ministry which relates on earth to the High Priesthood of Jesus Christ is that of the whole People of God. But in practice, their role is often usurped by sections of the church which claim specialist insights and authority. One example: pressure from Pope John Paul resulted in unusually harsh treatment of those involved in abortion in Poland. Doctors who performed abortions outside an extremely limited field could be jailed. The result? Police reported ten times the number of new-born babies discarded and left to die in rivers and rubbish tips. That is what is called pro-life. To be genuinely pro-life is no straightforward matter.

We can be instructed by the picture of the church as a body in 1 Corinthians 12. The functioning of the whole depends on the interplay of parts which are specially adapted to the role they have to fulfil. In matters of sexual conduct it is those who have appropriate skills and experience and who know the options offered in particular situations where decisions are called for, who can give an instructed lead.

It is a time for the priestly people to take the authority in matters of sexuality which is theirs, and put it to work.

Coming home*

When you cross the borders of the
desert and head for home
you do not want to turn back.
What you are heading for
is a place of belonging
a place where you can lay your body down.
Everything inside you is running
you have run away often
but this time you are running for home.

You will still be yourself
still be restless sometimes and afraid
but what beckons you now are
bonds of loving
and, when all is said and done
(and sometimes there is too much saying
and too little doing)
living where your life belongs
is coming home.
Welcome to the family.

* This poem was written for someone joining the church

Wild uncharted seas: sexuality and belonging

'We have left undone those things which we ought to
have done; we have done those things we ought not to
have done, and there is no health in us.'[1]

Thomas Cranmer's confession, though dated, is at least balanced.
When it comes to sexuality, however, the church over the ages has
managed to persuade us that there is only one kind of sin — that
of commission. Though there is little or nothing in the gospels to
convince us of the case, two thousand years of spirituality divorced
from our earthly selves has created a horrific split which has
divided our Self from ourself. In this view of the world, we are *all*
outsiders. We have responded by creating artificial barriers which
put some people more on the outside than others. The Approved
Self is divorced from its own material existence, and believes the
appetites of the body to be at best a nuisance in a particularly
pernicious way. As a thirteen-year-old choirgirl I was banned,
with the other girls, from a new vicar's induction service because
we 'distracted the men'. It was a shock to my whole psyche to
hear myself spoken of in this way — the first shock, but not the
last. Men have to tell their own story of what this has meant —
and many are doing so.

Mirfield father Harry Williams tells the story of his journey
from a split Self to wholeness in his autobiographical *Some Day
I'll Find You*. Early on in the book, he tells us: 'After all, as far as
my own life is concerned, what passes for virtue has been a far
more destructive force than what passes for vice.'[2] Acknowledging
his homosexuality, the years of denial, his inability to make 'the
single unique relationship with another'[3], he looks back with a
shudder on the times when, as a young priest, he toed the party
line. He wonders that his sister ever forgave him for the
sanctimonious letter written when she proposed to marry a
divorced man. Of the young man to whom he refused absolution
because the young confessor had no intention of giving up his
homosexual relationship, Williams writes:

I now only hope he disregarded everything I said. I had given no consideration whatever to the delicate, complicated, vulnerable humanity not only of my penitent but of his friend; nor had I taken into account the fact that real, genuine love, God's greatest gift in making us only a little lower than the angels, can find expression in an infinite variety of ways, including those which any particular culture may find unacceptable.[4]

Genuine love — delicate-complicated-vulnerable-infinite-variety — there can hardly be a paragraph in contemporary writing which more honestly sums up the nature of our sexuality. Far from being the height of evil, something to be rejected in our higher search for God, it is part of what makes us 'inferior only to the angels' *(Psalms 8:5)*. When I left Trinity College, Toronto, someone sent me a questionnaire about my 'spiritual formation' at the college. Was it regular attendance at Evensong which had done the trick? 'Other' kinds of prayer ... and so on. There was a space underneath for 'other' but not room to write what I really wanted to say. There are moments in church, and moments here and there when I glimpse God — but it's in the arms of my lover, in the heartstopping vulnerability of that moment, when I am loved and accepted for what I am, not what I pretend to be, that I know there is a God who *enjoys life.* In sexual expression I was able to make a dying man feel healed. If this is a pale shadow, what must the Real Thing be like!

Inheriting the whirlwind

And yet ... because our sexual nature, our hunger for being connected (literally) with another, is so powerful, it is so open to misuse. We have inherited a whirlwind when we search for sexual identity. How can we be a man in a world where men have used sexual and physical power to demean, oppress and kill women? How can we be a woman when women have learned to submit, to play act, to manipulate? How can we admit to our homosexuality when there is one, and only one, allowable form of sexual activity? How can we form heterosexual relationships once we know the multitude of sins hidden behind that door? There is little correlation between the name of our relationship ('marriage' or 'gay' or 'lesbian' or 'cohabiting') and the intrinsic goodness of it. Dare we admit that? Which came first — the distortion of sexuality by human sin, or the religious denunciation of our sexual beings?

Most of all, how can we give ourself to the other when we have been taught to hate, despise and hide our Self? No wonder the norm of sexual expression instead becomes furtive, smutty, full of innuendo, pornographic and downright sad, instead of genuinely and joyfully erotic. The erotic has been allowed no place in our spirituality, so our urgent and inescapable sexuality has been colonized by the Father of Lies. And yet many of our liturgies, and prayers, and other forms of 'spiritual' expression, are blatantly erotic — if only we could recognize it.

In the nineteenth century, Josephine Butler risked the opprobium of the entire Victorian establishment, of which she was an inheritor by birth, in her lifelong campaign against the Contagious Diseases Acts and the regulation of prostitution. She refused to be divided from her sisters who were forced into prostitution, or to accept that it was necessary for men to have this outlet for their 'natural appetites'. She spoke of the man who was shocked to find that the twelve-year-old procured for him by a brothel was his own daughter — anyone else's daughter would have done. After meeting the head of the Morals Police in Paris, and hear him denigrate the women of the streets, she said, 'And to think that I, a woman, should hear women thus spoken of to my face.'[5]

Like Harry Williams, she understood that we are all sisters and brothers under the skin — all called to the same vulnerable humanity, the same search for God the Creator. All of us have been hurt, to a greater or lesser degree, in this quest. We have painful stories to tell. That we keep trying is a miracle in itself.

And here's where the church should at least have the decency to get out of the way with its one-sided view. There are terrible sins of omission in the use of our sexuality. There's the refusal to be really vulnerable — there's sexual disdain, and withdrawal (emotional, spiritual, as well as physical). For every person whose sexual engagement is without consideration for the other, or for all the others in their life, there's one whose decision *not* to engage with another is as much about self-protection as about virtue.

A sense of dispossession

That's not to advocate a sexual free-for-all, but to plead for a way to create a new context for our sexuality — where it is part of our whole self, joyfully acknowledged in all our attractions and relationships with each other, physically expressed in various ways where our vulnerability will be treasured as God treasures it, contained in celibacy when that is our calling.

Harry Williams locates his 'sense of dispossession' in his discovery that 'I wanted evidently to belong not only to somebody else but also in some important way to the natural order.'[6]

It's that belonging which mystics like Julian of Norwich experience in their erotically expressed longing for God from a life of celibacy.

It is that belonging which Welsh poet Dannie Abse refers to in his 'Epithalamion'. Although he entitles this wonderful expression of very Celtic spirituality 'Wedding Song', it could be a song about all our sexuality, all our ways of yearning to be 'inferior only to the angels':

> For today I took to my human bed,
> Flower, and bird, and wind, and world,
> And all the living, and all the dead.[7]

What precarious idols, what artificial barriers, would we all have to break down, to make that belonging possible within our human experience?

---

* This chapter title, 'Wild, uncharted seas', was inspired by a verse from the song 'You and I' which Ewan McColl wrote for Peggy Seeger

Woman without a name*

Woman
without a name,
raped and abused
until break of day
then taken limb by limb
through the length of the land.
What symbolism is this?
What do I hear
in your silences?

Who questions your abuse
and the crime
against female sexuality
when the only question is misuse
of man's property?

Can I stand in solidarity
with your pain
and let the silence be
wordless?

Is your silence
louder than the cry
from the cross?

* This poem refers to text in Judges 19

Nightmares in the garden: Christianity and sexual violence

Jean's arms were twisted up behind her head, and tied tightly with nylon rope. She was blindfolded and gagged so she couldn't see or shout; but she knew what was going to happen next. Her bruised, bleeding body was nailed to the ground by the excruciating agony of anal rape. Her ears were assaulted by the endless, screaming insults. There was a burning emptiness at the core of her being.

Next morning, Jean and her husband washed and dressed, and attended church. He read a lesson about loving your enemies, and she organized a team of helpers for the coffee morning.

Linda is a competent professional woman who grieves deeply for the loss of the whole and happy person she might have been. Abused by an uncle throughout childhood and puberty, she blocked out the trauma until, as an adult, painful memories began to surface. She felt disturbed by unresolved issues about her identity and sexuality. As a Christian, she turned to her priest for support and counselling. He exploited her vulnerability, flattered her, and forced her into sexual behaviour which he claimed was part of God's healing. Nothing could have damaged her fragile integrity more, and now Linda struggles every day, as she has done for long, hard years, with depression, loneliness and the erosion of self-worth.

Miriam's first trick was when she was fourteen, and in care. A young guy at the school gate offered her money and clothes — and a little bit of affection — if she would go with men in cars. By the time she was sixteen, she was hooked on drugs and willing to do anything. She was terrified that her pimp would kill her. She cried every day, and drank every night. She got pregnant and had a botched abortion. At nineteen, she was in jail for soliciting.

Jean and Linda and Miriam, like millions of girls and women, grew up dreaming of Eden: of romance and tender love; of white weddings and living happily-ever-after. Instead, they have been hurt, degraded, abused and imprisoned by sexual violence.

For too long, there has been a conspiracy of silence about this global epidemic. In our own time and place, acts of incest, harassment, rape, inappropriate or non-consensual touching, verbal abuse and other kinds of violation have on the one hand been condemned as unnatural and monstrous; yet they have also been concealed, explained away, or blamed on the victims. This is especially true when they occur within that lawless realm known as marriage and family, where the façade of public respectability can conceal hideous private terrors. For centuries, sexuality — especially female sexuality — has been feared and reviled within the Christian church, which has sought to control erotic activity within narrow parameters. But just as we may at last be willing to acknowledge erotic and genital activity as legitimate sources of pleasure, goodness and creativity, we are confronted with increasing evidence of sexual danger: not that sense of risk and awe which can be a key element of erotic passion, but the destructive danger which attacks the physical, psychological and spiritual integrity of human beings. Is it an exaggeration to suggest that it is more common for sex to be experienced as a commodity; an instrument of abuse and alienation and control, than as an expression of mutual enjoyment? This dismal hypothesis is substantiated by evidence which recites a global and depressing litany of gender violence[1]:

- In Scotland, it is estimated that 40,000 women in Glasgow alone live in intimate relationships which include regular physical, sexual and emotional abuse
- In the USA:

  every fifteen seconds a woman is beaten

  every six minutes a woman is raped

  every day four women are killed by abusive men
- In parts of Africa, thousands of female children are routinely subjected to genital mutilation
- There is a large-scale global industry in the trafficking of women
- Sex tourism exploits and ruins the lives of countless girls and boys
- Rape is a war crime, used on a massive scale in Korea, Bosnia, Rwanda, the Gulf and other fields of conflict
- In Mexico, ninety-five per cent of women claim sexual harassment at work
- It is estimated that at least one in three female children (and

many male children too suffer some form of sexual abuse: usually at the hands of a known man

- Eight-five per cent of rapists are known to their victims, and sixty per cent of rapes are committed indoors — mostly in the woman's own home
- Homosexuals, lesbians, transsexuals are routinely subjected to vilification and discrimination: not least by the Christian church

Under a thin veneer of normality, the sheer scale and extent of such abuse creates a climate of vulnerability and fear which shapes the daily experience and relationships of us all. Each time a woman is afraid to go out at night; or a man is wary about showing affection to his daughter; or a woman squirms in silent embarrassment at her colleague's offensive comments; or an abused child is too frightened to tell what is happening, witness is borne to the deep distortions at the very heart of our corporate life.

Self-understanding, relationships, roles and structures within Western societies are deeply influenced by the Judeo-Christian tradition. Many victims, survivors and perpetrators of sexual violence are practising Christians. What are the connections between sexuality, gender, eroticism and violence in our religious heritage? Is it possible for those who have been hurt, disillusioned and damaged to hold on to that dream of Eden? Perhaps, instead, the question should be, is it desirable? Was it all so sweet and lovely in the garden of earthly delights — or is it time to wake up from a nightmare?

'Woodstock' was Canadian singer Joni Mitchell's elegiac tribute to the spirit of the 1960s. In that song, the famous music festival symbolizes the attempts of a generation to overturn the rigid conventions and injustices which had characterized post-war attitudes to sexuality and politics. The refrain conveys a yearning for a time of innocence and love:

> We are starlight, we are golden, and we got to get ourselves back to the Garden[2]

What a lovely image, and didn't it seem like the most natural thing in the world to want get back to that place where a man and a woman could be naked without shame? The 'sexual revolution' indeed wrought many significant and positive changes, but surely all but the most myopic or self-centred flower children must view its achievements with a measure of cynicism, in the context of the harsh evidence about sexual abuse. For perhaps it wasn't so revolutionary, but depended on an ancient and tenacious myth of human relationship: tantalizingly romantic on the surface, but dangerous and damaging at the core. What really went on in the Garden of Eden? Was Eve framed?

The story of Adam and Eve in the Garden of Eden lies at the heart of Christian theology, traditions and attitudes to gender and sexuality. From Paul to Phyllis Tribble, biblical commentators, church fathers, ecumenical councils, Popes, reformers, synods, assemblies and ordinary Christians, have studied, interpreted, and appealed to the story. Individuals, societies and cultures have been constructed accordingly. So we inhabit a world of potent, jostling images of sexual interaction, where some children can watch Snow White simper 'Some day my prince will come', while others (or even the same ones) are forced to perform genital acts for the erotic pleasure of apparently respectable adults.

According to the traditional interpretations of Genesis 2-3, the Garden of Eden was a pleasant paradise of sufficiency, security, protection, care, innocence and companionship; until the poison of disobedience and sin seeped in. Then the first human beings were given due punishment: labour and toil for Adam, longing and subjection for Eve. And so the fallen world, tainted with sexual fear, lust and the power of men over women, has become prey to exploitation and violence. Well, that's the story, and it's been imprinted deep onto the minds, hearts and bodies of women and men. But what if that subjection followed from the rationale of Eden itself; and what if that myth, of man and woman; husband and wife; two people, one flesh, eternally united as God and nature intended, has been a basic source of sexual violence?

What characterized the relationship of Adam and Eve in the primal, innocent romance? According to centuries of Christian readings, there were three fundamental elements:

> Eve was created *after* Adam
> Eve was created *from* Adam
> Eve was created *for* Adam

The idea that women were, by divine purpose, derivative and ancillary, enters into the Christian tradition through Paul (1 Corinthians 11), who proposes a hierarchy of order, headship and glory in the image of God. Women reflect the likeness of God, not in themselves, but only through men: 'He for God only, she for God in Him.'[3] Eve was brought into being, not for her intrinsic worth, but to 'help' Adam. She was constructed out of Adam's side, and he assumed the right to name her as such. And what was the point of making her? Augustine struggled with that conundrum:

> If it is necessary for one of two people living together to rule and the other to obey so that an opposition of wills does not disturb their peaceful cohabitation, then nothing is missing from the order we see in Genesis directed to this restraint, for one person was created before, the other afterwards, and most significantly, the latter was created from the former, the woman from the man. And nobody wants to suggest, does he, that God, if he so willed, could only make a woman from a man's side, yet that he couldn't create a man as well? I cannot think of any reason for woman's being made as man's helper, if we dismiss the reason of procreation.[4]

Other theologians may not have gone that far, but the overwhelming consensus of the tradition was that women were, as one seventeenth-century cleric put it, 'vessels for use'.[5] Their original and enduring function was to minister to the requirements and desires of men.

One humanity, two sexes: woman made for man. In Christian theology, sexual duality and complementarity has been presented as the natural order. Only by accepting their radical difference and distinctive functions could men and women fulfil the divine intent. As countless people have discovered to their cost, any departure from this prescribed norm was regarded as deviant and monstrous. Compulsory heterosexuality has proclaimed other modes of sexual expression to be deviant, and therefore subject to censure. Gender complementarity has, historically, declared that women who refuse to conform to their prescribed roles in relation to men, were monstrous. They dared to step out of the tightly confined and controlled 'woman's sphere', and could be chastised accordingly. The branks, a common post-reformation Scottish punishment for 'unruly women', was a painful iron mask which was designed specifically to make the wearer look like a hideous monster. And still, in contemporary Britain, women are confronted with regular reminders that they are alien, unwelcome invaders in male space. There have been many alarming cases of sustained sexual harassment and abuse of women in traditionally male environments: the fire service, the police, the Houses of Parliament, the church.

The tyranny of dualism in Western thought and culture has been well documented, especially by feminists. Supported by research in the human sciences of biology and genetics, they argue that the idea of two sharply differentiated sexes is largely a social creation, unsupported by any natural order, and requiring constant vigilance and coercion for its maintenance. It is not difference *per se*, but the way that difference is used to systematize subordination, which has normalized the possibility of violence and abuse in gender relations. The story of Adam and Eve, as archetype and model of God's order, has embedded gender dualism in our social and ethical arrangements, by presenting it, not as a matter of cultural construction, kept in place by human convention and decision, but as inescapably *natural*, and therefore beyond the scope of human manipulation or revision.

What is the connection between this, and the reality of sexual violence? If romantic love is based on the religious theory that it is natural for a sacrificial, loyal, enclosing female nature to *complement* a self-possessing and masterful male nature (and it is not just trashy Barbara Cartland fiction which extols this), then sexual desire becomes associated with the self-destruction of subordination and the self-aggrandisement of domination. Men become real men by overwhelming, penetrating, possessing and controlling women. Women become proper women by submitting and serving. The Old Testament's 'texts of terror'[6] are all about women as instruments who can be used, abused, then discarded, forgotten or killed. But the legitimate marriage relationship, as described in the Law and history of the Jewish people, exhibited many of the same features: men 'took' wives as part of their economic wealth. Adultery was essentially a crime against another man's property. Wives had no rights of possession over their own physical or sexual integrity. This has been a widespread cross-cultural reality: until very recently, the possibility of rape in marriage has not been recognized in Scots or English Law. Even scriptural uses of the marriage metaphor to describe the relationship between God and humankind are based on models of patriarchy not mutuality.

In keeping with this 'natural order', the Pope saw fit to exhort thousands of Bosnian women who had been victims of war rape not to have abortions, while his counsel was supported by an Italian newspaper which praised the 'womanhood whose wondrous passivity was made to pardon, accept, nourish, procure, nurture and protect — lovingly sacrificing herself'.[7] And Karl Barth, so convinced that the ethics of divine command required unconditional female submission, suggested that if women remain quiet and obedient in the face of male oppression or violence, this would win men to repentance for their misdeeds.[8] Such is the pathological advice which has given comfort to so many abusive men in home, church and community, while burdening their victims with the hopeless task of responsibility for changing bad male behaviour. The truth is that women — in marriage and other institutions — have been treated as shock absorbers, endlessly expected to give up their own living space, to accept and conceal the marks of possession on their bodies, minds and spirits.

Before the Fall, Eve's immortal perfection lay in her limitation and subordination. Most of the men who have shaped Christian culture and theology believed that her submission to Adam preceded the expulsion from the Garden. Indeed, that momentous conclusion to the story of Eden was the dreadful consequence of independent female action, while Adam's sin was sometimes characterized as simply being foolish (or affectionate) enough to listen to Eve's advice, when he should have rebuked her for attempting to subvert his God-given authority. According to some of the 'devil books' (*Teufelbücher*) which were so popular in sixteenth-century Protestant Germany, pandering to men obsessed by a fear of 'masterless' women, poor old Adam was merely the first henpecked husband (he was called *Siemann* — that is 'she-man'). Ever since Eden, Satan had been intent on attacking the 'natural order' of male dominance and female obedience. The Scottish reformer John Knox was particularly vehement about the curse which befell Eve:

> For where before thy obedience should have been voluntary, now it shall be by constraint and by necessity, and that because thou hast deceived thy man, thou shalt therefore be no longer mistress over thine own appetites, over thine own will, nor desires ... He shall be lord and governor, not only over thy body, but even over thy appetites and will.[9]

It is not hard to see in this world view, the centrality of a theological model based on a hierarchy of obedience and submission: man submits to God, woman submits to man, nature submits to humankind, and control can be exercised by force, if required. This ethos of domination and dependence has served to legitimize patriarchal power in home, church and public life, and has often given blessing to coercion of those perceived as subordinate. At the apex of this chain of command stands God — a deity traditionally spoken of in male language and understood as judgemental, omnipotent, sometimes capricious and apparently entitled to overrule accepted moral codes of appropriate behaviour, to fulfil his divine purpose. One of John Donne's *Holy Sonnets* makes striking use of imagery which clearly derives from the experience and language of courtship and marital relationships. God here is like men who can love and act violently 'for her own good', with the same easy hand:

> Batter my heart, three-personed God, for you
> As yet but knock, breathe, shine and seek to mend
> That I may rise and stand, o'erthrow me and bend
> Your force to break, blow, burn and make me new
> I, like an usurped town to another due,
> Labour to admit you, but O, to no end.
> Reason, your viceroy in me, me should defend,
> But is captived and proves weak or untrue.
> Yet dearly I love you and would be loved fain
> But am betrothed unto your enemy.
> Divorce me, untie, or break that knot again,
> Take me to you, imprison me, for I,
> Except you enthrall me, never shall be free,
> Nor ever chaste except you ravish me.

Control, possession, mastery: these are the characteristics of unequal and distorted power relations. They have been expressed in the battering, bending, breaking and burning of women, children and 'deviant' men. They have been used to imprison and ravish under the guise of romance and love and marriage. They have eroticized violence. Some religious men have admitted, and gloried in their power. This man habitually beat and raped his wife:

> Yes, that's what it is ... strength ... and like really feeling your strength. It's the same feeling you get standing in front of a congregation, you know, having them in the palm of your hand ... First with some resistance, and then suddenly you have them, and they're caught. And it's sort of the same thing sexually ... you somehow conquer the resistance. That's the fantastic thing, it's like a victory, you get the upper hand, you have the power to conquer that which has been closed to you ... It is not for nothing that we men were made in God's image.[10]

Of course, not all personal relationships between men and women are like this. Plenty of people enjoy the pleasure — carnal and otherwise — of mutual regard, affection, excitement and respect for space, integrity, freedom. But these features can be present in fleeting moments, or enduring over a period of time; they can be part of friendships between people in different combinations of gender and sexual orientation. They can inhere in networks of relationship which stretch and break the traditional dualities. Love, friendship and justice are often part of formal marriage; but so are pain and humiliation and destruction. Genital sex can be awkward, boring or unpleasant between people who deeply care for one another; it can also be a delightful expression of physical compatibility with one to whom no lasting commitment has been made. The church has concentrated on the functionality of sex, and largely condemned any experience or relationship which does not conform to the exclusive sexual property contract of heterosexual marriage. It has attended to the outward form, rather than the quality, of sexual relationships; obsessed with condemning 'immoral' acts, regardless of their consensual and positive potential. But the church has also colluded in the silence surrounding violence and abuse which is an all-too-regular outcome in the privatized realm upon which it bestows exclusive blessing. I agree with Marvin Ellison, who appeals for a Christian sexual ethics based on the principle of 'common decency', and writes:

> Marriage retains its value and meaning, not as a 'licence for sex' or declaration of possession, but as one possible framework of accountability, and secure place to form durable bonds of devotion, affection, intimacy. These should be expected to strengthen persons to deepen ties of affection and friendship beyond as well as within the primary relation, rather than fostering control and dependency.[11]

Sadly, the Christian tradition has largely failed to grasp the connection between personal, sexual, economic and social wellbeing. Sexual distortion and exploitation too often mirror the larger realities of alienation and prejudice and sexual pleasure is not enough, in itself, to restore the widespread damage done to human self-worth by unjust actions, systems or structures.

Let's get back to the Garden. For most of Christian history, the choice for women seems to have been the pleasant submission of Eden, or the penal subjection of the Fall. Women have been, and continue too often to be constructed:

- *after* men (so they are named and viewed from a central male perspective)
- *from* men (so they have been denied the right truly to define their own identity)
- *for* men (so their value is assessed according to how well they fulfil their serving roles)

We may decide that the story of the Garden has caused more damage to the formation of human relationships than can be repaired by any amount of alternative exegesis, however ingenious. But it's good to dream, and if we need sources of encouragement and insight to challenge sexual violence, perhaps another visit to Eden will offer new fruits to nourish us.

The old view of paradise bound men and women to the inevitability of a 'natural order', and the colonizing logic of mastery. But another path takes us on a journey of growing awareness, maturity and responsibility. The garden is a secure and protected environment: a place of delight and the innocence of children who are unaware of all the complex forces which are integral to God's creation. But the garden also contains the potential for knowledge and wisdom and change — symbolized by water, trees, fruits, the serpent. And Eve's initiative is an assertion that it is time to move from the simple dependence of unquestioning infancy, to a more realistic and mature capacity for engaging with God. Through her actions, the world is revealed as so much larger and ambiguous than Eden, and those who are imprinted with the image of God, have to take responsibility for working, not just to understand their personal or sexual identity, but to construct complex communities of connection between all created things. We should not be bound by the stereotypes and exaggerations of difference, but find creative and just ways to affirm our glorious diversity. In our freedom, we have to cope with suffering and death; we must acknowledge our limitations and interdependence. But if we can struggle free from the trappings of false romanticism, if we can subvert the latent sexual violence of imposed gender roles, perhaps we might discover what it really means to be faithful lovers. This is our unfinished human task and delight.

Man to (wo)man

I can't
atone for centuries
of misuse
I can't
condone
ongoing abuse
I can't
be liable
every time
I can't be tryable
for every crime
I can't become
what you are
clearly
but I can
listen
and learn
and change
and grow
so
please
don't
give up on me
quite yet.

The lost boys: the impact of feminism and gay thought on male heterosexuality

For many heterosexual men, the 1990s represent a decade of insecurity and fear about their identity. The traditional role for men, that of being the breadwinner for the family, is in terminal decline. Women now form the main or only income for an increasing number of families. As a result of this change in the role of men in society, there has been a growing sense of crisis in men's lives. Young males seem to be struggling to fit into this apparently fragmenting society. One painful development of this struggle for identity is a dramatic rise in suicides among young males. Another development has been the increase in reports showing apparent drops in male sperm levels, raising the possibility of serious infertility problems in the years to come. It is not a good time to be male.

I would like to offer a very personal reflection on my experience as a heterosexual male at the end of the twentieth century. In the course of this reflection I want to touch upon the influence of feminism and gay theology, as I see it, upon being male. I want to offer a personal view of the apostle Peter, and through this explore a possible aspect of male emotional development.

Beginnings of the author

I was born in Stobhill Hospital, Glasgow, in 1969. I was raised, firstly, in the Milton area of the city, and then later on in the Glasgow overspill town of Erskine in Renfrewshire. My early childhood was fairly normal, as far as I can remember it. I was an only child. One of my earliest memories, aged five or six, concerned recognizing a difference between my parents. This was in terms of their roles within the family rather than in terms of their sexuality. I noticed that my dad would come in from his work as a bus driver, hard work that involved him sitting down all day in his cab. He would take off his jacket and sit down. I would then notice that my mum would come from being a cleaner, on her feet and sometimes her knees all day, and she would start working again. Nothing dramatic happened in my consciousness, I just remember thinking how unfair that seemed on my mum. Why should she have to do all the work in the house, while my father was allowed to sit down and relax? At that time this experience taught me that my father must be the head of the family while my mum was the helper to the head. It was only later, during my painful teenage years, when my relationship with my father was practically over and my family seemed to be in a time of difficulty, that I was able to see the reality of my parents' identity. I saw that my mother was, in actual fact, the strongest member of the family, and therefore, its natural head, who, through hard work, strength and determination kept the family going. Without her, there would have been no family.

My first real introduction to feminism came when I was a student at the University of Edinburgh. One of my friends was a very strong and passionate feminist. I can remember going to one of Edinburgh's well-known bookshops. We went to the 'Woman's Section', as my friend wanted to buy a particular book. I remember being completely dumbfounded at the size of the section and at the breadth of the subjects under the heading of 'Feminism'. I had no idea, no knowledge of any of this. I felt jealous at these resources, almost a feeling of jealousy at the experiences described within these books. I felt jealous because, as a man, I had no language, no resources such as these to articulate my situation. The only thing open to me, as a heterosexual man, was the traditional male way of expression, namely self-abuse, through alcoholism, violence or silence. I chose silence. I was not easy to be with. I was left with many doubts and feelings of shame at my male identity.

Feminism as a liberation movement for humanity

My introduction to feminism also provided a beginning, enabling me to start looking at my own life, my own identity as a man. Feminism confronted me with a profound picture of male abuse of power. Feminism, it seemed to me, also offered women a new paradigm of understanding, in which their experience was defined on their own terms, and not by men. It argued very strongly that the personal is political and that the political is also the personal. I thought of my mother and of how it seemed that her personal identity was removed by taking on the identity and emotions of the family, of both my father and myself. I thought of my girlfriends, who would end up dealing with my emotional pain in the same way my mother previously had. I thought of my female friends who had been attacked and threatened and raped by other men. I realized at this point that my contact with feminism had led to changes in my thinking. And yet I was still not able to express what I thought a man should be, nor was I able to express my own male identity.

I passionately believe that the feminist movement is one of the most liberating movements ever to have been established in the history of humanity. I believe that feminism has brought about a paradigm shift in the world's history and development and has introduced a real presence of liberation into the lives of women all over the world.

I want to argue, in the light of my experience, that feminism can also be a liberating movement for men. I believe that it is the questioning and rejection of patriarchy, a world view that distorts the humanity of men as well as women, that holds the beginning of the long process to liberate men. A process that men must undertake on their own. Feminism can, I believe, provide a starting point for men, allowing them to begin to understand themselves. This process can begin against the background of what I believe is the fundamental reality and truth of feminism as a liberative movement.

I believe that some men have already rejected patriarchy. This rejection is expressed in a rejection of themselves. It is expressed in their lack of ability to use language to describe their emotions and feelings. This lack of emotional expression, of the ability to have real intimacy with themselves and with others, has led to very real and painful breakdowns and depression. I want to look at this later on, through the eyes of Peter.

Gay role models

My time studying at the Union Theological Seminary in the City of New York was the first time that I had ever lived with gay men. On arrival, discovering that I was one of the few 'straight' men on my floor in the halls of residence, I was initially quite frightened. I had previously regarded myself as one of the most liberal acceptors of gay males. I was forced to take a second look at my beliefs in the light of my fear at being in this situation. I was terrified of being taken for a gay man. I was terrified of having my sexuality questioned or presumed. On reflection, I was terrified of having my whole identity, sexual and spiritual, reduced to being a sexual object; exactly the same emotions and feelings that millions of women have experienced in their relationships with heterosexual men. My fear appeared during my first week, and disappeared quite quickly at the beginning of the second week when my floor mates, being mature, reasoned human beings, were completely accepting of my heterosexuality. However the experience of my reaction had a profound effect on my thinking and development as a heterosexual male.

I found at Union a community of articulate, welcoming, bright gay, lesbian and bisexual Christians who were having to deal with oppression, hatred and judgement on an almost weekly basis. They represented to me yet another group of human beings who have had a particularly horrific time at the hands of heterosexual men.

The gay men that I got to know at Union were truly strong men. They had come through many years of pain, self-doubt and searching. They had endured many painful rejections from close family and friends, tearing themselves apart in the process. However, they were able to find the strength from somewhere and were able to keep going. During the course of many years spent struggling, they had developed a deep, strong understanding of what it meant to be a gay man. They had developed a spirituality that spoke of what it means to be rejected, not on the grounds of their personal identity, but on the grounds of their sexual identity. They also had a wonderfully liberative sense of being male, which was a highly positive identity for them, and something worthy of much praise and celebration.

This made a big impression on me. The feeling of acceptance, of brotherhood and sisterhood was very strong, as was the communion and spirituality. To Paul's famous declaration of the revolution of Jesus, I would add the phrase, 'There is no gay or straight, all are one in Christ Jesus.' What is it about us heterosexual males that we hate those who are different from us?

My experience at Union was another major influence on my search for understanding and language that had its beginning in that Edinburgh bookshop many years earlier. It taught me that men can be emotional and open. That men can let go of power, of the fear that our lives are meaningless and our identities lost. It taught me that these developments can happen in the lives of heterosexual men, but only after a long period of pain and searching.

Peter the rock

Peter is probably the disciple to whom I feel closest. In the gospels he comes across as a headstrong, impulsive, fearful, emotional man. He seems very real to me; one of the most real people in the Bible. The gospels present Simon Peter as a tough, hard-working fisherman, with little in the way of any formal education. He seemed to have everything: a job, a family. And yet he gave up everything to follow Jesus. What was it about Jesus that made Simon Peter leave the security of his life? How did his friends and family react? Perhaps they thought that he had finally lost the place, all those nights fishing in the Sea of Galilee had messed with his brain. Or perhaps Simon Peter had been fumbling all his life for a meaning that filled an aching gap in his life, a gap that he could find no words to describe. Was Jesus able to offer this tough, working-class fisherman a real sense of intimacy for the first time in his life? When you think about the calling of Simon Peter by Jesus, it must have been either an incredibly brave thing to do, or a very stupid thing. The gospel writers describe this part of the story very simply. They do not share the hesitations, the doubts, the insecurities, of which there must have been many. This was a massive life change for Simon Peter.

Three developments take place within Simon Peter's story that offer wee clues to his sense of identity. The first is receiving a new name from Jesus. He goes from Simon the fisherman, to Peter, the rock. This seems to come out of nowhere. The standard, traditional reading of this event might see it as a sign that Simon Peter's masculinity has been endorsed and confirmed. Peter is a real man. In renaming Simon as Peter the rock, Jesus is praising Peter, not only as the leader of men, but also as the founder of the church. Well, that's not how I see it. I see a much more human, vulnerable picture of a nervous, shy but honest man. A man who continually struggles to deal with all that has happened to him since meeting Jesus. I think Peter's first reaction to his naming is to be slightly embarrassed. Perhaps he is frightened that he will never be able to fully live up to this new identity, this new role.

One of the first actions of this new solid rock is to attempt to walk towards Jesus on the water. With a rush of blood to the head, he is the first out of the boat, only to start sinking when he notices what he is actually doing. This is a wonderful picture of Peter's impulsiveness and his devotion for Jesus. The rock only too quickly makes people aware of his jelly feet.

The third story about Peter that I want to focus on is the moment when everything becomes a nightmare for him. It is probably the most important moment of his life. A chance for him to show his love and loyalty for Jesus. When the moment arrives, Peter the rock crumbles into a thousand pieces. The story is the arrest of Jesus. After Jesus' arrest in the garden, the disciples scatter to the four winds. All, except of course the women, who prove to be, without exception, the strongest and most faithful of Jesus' companions and disciples. Peter hovers around on the edge of things, trying to be anonymous. When suddenly, some of the stardom of being the rock comes back to haunt him, and he gets recognized. The rest of the story is very well-known and as the cock crows for the third and final time, Peter is utterly alone as his personal nightmare develops apace. Peter is in total agony, broken, shattered, destroyed. Some rock. Some man.

Perhaps this is the point which many men today feel that they have reached. Everything that used to provide an identity, a meaning, has become rather inadequate now. Many men seem to have no release, other than self-abuse, or abuse of others around them. They seem to have no language in which to express themselves, other than a painful silence. Perhaps that is why so many young men, faced with this future, faced with the breakdown in their relationships with their fathers, end up attempting to kill themselves. Perhaps. Maybe the hardest question to answer is also one of the simplest: what does it mean to be a man? Older generations of men might be able to answer this question more easily than mine. They might reflect on the importance of getting a 'good job' in providing a real sense of meaning and identity. This is closely bound to the role the of breadwinner and of meeting the 'right woman' and starting a family. Or then again, they might simply answer the question by replying that to be a man means 'not being a woman', as if that is somehow self-explanatory. Hey presto! We've found the answer, call off the search. How do you attempt to articulate a theology, a sense of spirituality, for a group of human beings who have no idea who they are?

In Peter's case, the effect of his deep trauma is to make him dissolve into tears, into a rejection of himself and a deep depression. A very familiar male reaction. All the insecurities and fears, the self-doubts and low self-esteem come flooding out. All his feelings of love and intimacy that developed through his contact with Jesus seem to be broken. And yet the ending of this story is very well known. Three days later, life's heartbeat restarts. The Master, the dreamer, the lover of women and men, brings transformation and healing to the human race. To the disciples this transformation must have been remarkable. And yet, there is in Peter's story a sense that the Resurrection of Jesus did not provide all the answers. Later on, after the Resurrection, we find the disciples sitting on the beach, when Peter makes the decision to go fishing. He decides to return to his former life, the way of life he had before he knew Jesus. He has grown tired of the emotional upheaval of the previous months. He wants some emotional stability and to find that he returns to his former life. Peter, or should that be Simon, is in the boat when a familiar story starts to replay itself before his eyes. A stranger appears and instructs the fishermen to try for fish on the other side of the boat. Imagine Peter's reaction as he hears those words. They immediately take him back to the beginning of everything. What happens next is, I think, one of the most tender healing stories in the Bible. Jesus asks this broken man, this man with no identity, if he loves him more than anyone else. Jesus asks the question three times, one for each of the denials. Jesus gives Peter forgiveness and healing, he gives Peter an opportunity to attempt to forgive himself. He is able to meet Peter where he is, in his pain and suffering. He offers Peter the chance to speak of this pain. Jesus shows Peter that his long dark night of fear and insecurity has been worth it. For in his brokenness and doubt, in his tears and denial, in his love and healing, Peter has become a rock.

Faith in the future?

This has been a very personal journey looking at my thoughts on feminism and my awareness of gay male perspectives and the impact of these on my life and on my faith. It is not meant to be a universal journey that is applicable to all; indeed I feel that an important aspect of the search for male identity is precisely that it can be conducted on a personal basis, that it can be fluid and changing, able to adapt to different circumstances and different understandings, something that is perhaps lacking in more traditional ideas of masculinity.

I believe that the future for heterosexual men is a long, hard and difficult one. There are no easy answers, no quick fixes. There is, I believe, only more doubt and anguish and pain. However I believe that this is necessary. Only when heterosexual men realize the reality of their situation will anything positive happen. Only when heterosexual men realize that women control their own destinies, that they are not there to be mothers and lovers and emotional stabilizers for men, will anything positive happen. Only when heterosexual men learn to accept difference, learn to let go of the power that they think they hold, become more open to their emotions, and gain the ability to learn and listen from their feminist sister and their gay brother, will anything positive happen. Only when heterosexual men are able to stop and listen to themselves, to confront the silence and the fear within, will anything positive happen. It is not about becoming new men. Peter can never be described as a new man. Peter's relationship with Jesus shows that the true man within Peter was always known to Jesus. In my opinion, it is about becoming real men, in the sense of letting go, opening up, and learning that we have to do it ourselves. It is also about accepting who we are and learning from the world around us.

If we can find the strength to enter the dark night of our souls, we might find a way through, a way to explore, confront and accept male spirituality and identity in our changing world.

Watchers at the gate*

At Gethsemane the skirts of light
grow wider in the immense dark,
revealing watchers at the gate.

The women there — watching, seeing,
awake: waiting without interfering
quiet in their humble love.

While sleeping men no longer attend,
the women focus wholly
on the depths of human experience.

Helpless, baffled, marginalized,
with a precious generosity
they minister with ears and eyes.

They are waiting with patient attention
for the insight not yet given;
waiting and never relinquishing

the ability to feel; never losing
the capacity for compassion
or the strength to hope;

waiting and holding on to their vision;
forever at the gate;
forever ready.

*Legend tells that when the apostles slept in the Garden of Gethsemane (Matthew 26:38) when Jesus asked them to stay awake and pray, Mary and Martha were awake, watching and praying at the Garden gate.

Flame within my being: incarnating feminist theology

I was slow to explore feminist theology, principally because I was afraid it might destroy something precious. God has always been around for me, for as long as I can remember. From childhood, God seemed to me to be important, necessary and welcome, and prayer a natural way of communicating my thoughts and feelings to God. Being brought up in a Scottish Christian home, there were of course ways of thinking about and praying to God which were taught and lived out, but although I went along with these, they never seemed to me wholly satisfactory.

Sunday worship always seemed perfectly adequate, and even enjoyable, but often failed to touch me. Men played the major roles in leading and organizing worship, and were deferred to; the activities of men (disciples, tax gatherers, fishermen, lawyers) seemed central to most gospel stories; and Paul's teaching and interpretation of Christ's life taken as a standard. I had no particular objection to any of this, except that it didn't often seem to correlate with my experience.

This was a theology and a religion to be grasped with the intellect. Somehow I wanted to experience and express the awesomeness of God in the infinitely deep night sky, fear of God in the dangerously powerful sea, joy to God in moments of piercingly tender love, despair to God in the midst of inexplicable abandonment — and not always in words. Colour, music, silence, gesture, seemed to me gifted for this. God seemed, and seems to me, so mysterious and yet so present that the most important prayer for me came to be the desire simply to know God more fully.

And so, like many women, I suspect, I lived a double life. 'Over the centuries, women have kept the church going by their faithfulness, but have lived their inner lives round its edges.'[1] Publicly, I went along with the conventions of a Christian who was trying to live a faithful life, and pushing down the questions about why I found it difficult to experience God in the way that other people seemed to do. Privately, I explored the idea of being transformed by God, and I expressed that in contemplative prayer. At this stage, I did not make any connections between gender difference and different experiences of God. Like many women, I felt it must be my fault in some way that I found it so difficult to connect with ordinary Christianity, and unfortunately some well-meaning men, in an attempt to help, simply reinforced this.

I coped with this double-life by having a spiritual director with whom I talked over my questions, and gradually came to have greater confidence in my own contemplative experience of God as being valid if not orthodox. Spirituality became more important to me than religion.

About ten years ago, however, I was becoming increasingly aware of the impact of feminist theology on my women friends. I resisted being drawn in because I thought then that tinkering with images of God and changing language didn't really address the difficulties. I was so habituated to the doublethink of mentally adjusting language and ritual to excuse the fact that it was exclusive of women that I had almost persuaded myself that theology could say one thing but really mean another. The situation became acute for me with the publication of Daphne Hampson's book, *Theology and Feminism*, which caused a commotion and drew some of my friends and acquaintances into the public debate. I began to feel I could not duck the issue any longer, and rather reluctantly began to read her book.

This tentative step changed my life. I had been fearful that feminist theology would present me with an understanding of God which would undermine completely my own painful groping towards the same thing — and undermine it so effectively that I would be unable to recover anything of God from the abyss. I was already insecure about my ability to sign up to the complete works of Christianity, still guilty about my own inability to talk confidently about meeting Jesus on life's journey. It sounds naïve, but I was convinced that if I couldn't find some compromise with the Christian church and my own experience I would lose my faith.

The gift that Hampson's book gave me was the insight that I could still believe in God and the power of prayer even if I were to cut adrift from a conventional belief system. This freed me to look at what my years of experiencing God had shown me to be true. It was one of the most profoundly liberating moments of my spiritual journey! Reading the final chapter of the book, in which Hampson affirms her continuing belief in God and the power of prayer, whilst rejecting conventional Christianity, was so powerful that I felt as if I had been struck in the chest. And in some ways, it did turn out to be like having my faith shock-started, and eventually brought to life in a new way.

I went on to read further, and to pick apart some of the early assumptions I had made about the nature of Christian belief. In parallel with this I continued to reflect spiritually about my own experience of God in prayer and relationships. This process of deconstruction was painful and eventually led me to the point where all I felt able to affirm was God, and the responsive relationship of prayer with God. This emptying out was an important precursor to being filled anew by God with an expanded awareness of the wonder of God's presence.

During this process, I began meeting up with four other women, not all of whom were convinced of the argument of feminist theology. We met to explore our feelings and convictions as women who believe in God and in our equality before God, and who wanted if possible to find some way of expressing that in our daily lives, in private prayer and in public worship. We talked a great deal but resolved very little! The group disbanded after a couple of years, but recently I got in touch with them again to ask, 'What impact has feminist theology had on you?'

The first of the women, Rebecca, had explored feminist theology when she was writing about the educational possibilities for women in the church. Not surprisingly she came to the conclusion that adult education for women in a church context was inadequate at best, and where any further education was offered, it took little account of women's concerns. There was little sensitivity to inclusive language, affirming women's experience of God (for example, in childbirth) and acknowledging the hidden existence of abuse. Rarely were there attempts to help women, and especially women who had not had the opportunity of further education, to make the important connections between faith and their life experiences.

So deeply was she disillusioned by this discovery, and by the unhelpful reaction of her own minister to her attempts to share some of her observations with him, that she has left the church. This is a source of regret to her, not least because she feels that the contact with a religious and hopefully spiritual community is lacking for her children, and she is unsure how to pass on to them some understanding of the spiritual tradition which still underpins her way of life. Inasmuch as God is still present for her, but the church is not, she would like to find some way of exploring and sharing her spirituality in community with others.

The second friend, Esther, came to the group having written a book on feminine aspects of God, so we reckoned she must have it sorted. She was so intrigued by the upsurge of ideas in feminist theology she subsequently decided she had to go right back to the roots and is now coming to the end of a course of study in one of the traditional theology colleges. Having been to the heart of masculine theology, she confessed that it was with a sense of relief that she could recover feminist theology and affirm its importance for her own spiritual life. Why the sense of relief? Like me, in relation to worship, she had been doing the double-think exercise for much of her time at college. Even well-meaning and otherwise sensitive male lecturers continue to speak from masculine experience as normative. For both of us, and probably for many women, a feminist understanding of God is not an alternative theology — an interesting idea to play with — it is integral to full theological understanding.

The third friend, Ruth, has shifted her position since the group disbanded. At that time she was not especially engaged by the feminist movement in the church — now she is an active supporter of Catholic women's ordination. Although she herself does not wish to be ordained, she now believes change to be essential and she sees it as having to come from within the institution. By supporting the movement she is making a statement for positive change, in the same way that she supported the anti-apartheid movement. She commented that in her opinion the church would be bankrupt without women, who have supported it, and not least financially, over the centuries, and if women stopped to think about the injustice of that position, many of them might simply leave.

The fourth woman, Deborah, is a single parent with two teenage children. She converted to Roman Catholicism, but this significant gesture has not always met with understanding or sympathy by the priests who minister to her worship community. Nuclear families are still normative, it seems, with many men who have decided they cannot combine close relationships with careers. Yet somehow as a divorced mother she combines full-time working with creating a happy and welcoming home for her children, with no support from a partner. Her experience of feminist theology has helped to free her from guilt — the guilt that is often inappropriately carried by women when their lives do not conform to other people's ideals. Like Ruth, she now actively supports the movement for women's ordination, and I suspect that this allegiance owes something to the undramatic but persistent lack of understanding she has met in ordained men.

So where does that leave the five of us? Feminist theology has had a profound impact on all our lives; perhaps by accident, since if theology had been properly integrated in the first place, none of us would have felt the need to campaign for the acceptance of a distinctively feminist version.

We have all recognized the far-reaching implications of accepting feminist theology: a fracture with the Christian tradition in which we have been nurtured and nourished, however inadequately. For many feminists this has meant a complete break, but some of us find ourselves lacking the courage, and perhaps the conviction, for such a decisive step. It is, after all, a community where we still find beloved companions amongst men as well as women. Rebecca, however, who has perhaps given the situation the most focused thought, has left the church and regrets the loss of contact with a spiritual community for herself and her children. Esther has changed churches several times and still finds it hard to find a place where she feels affirmed as a woman. Ruth and Deborah are now working for change within their branch of the institutional church for the affirmation of women's ministry which has been ruled out of order by their church authority.

For myself, I continue to go to church as a gesture of solidarity with people I love; but it is rarely a spiritual experience, and frequently seems disconnected from the things that concern me. Many of these would be labelled 'political'. I deplore the increasing gap between the rich who systematically accrue wealth at the expense of the poor. I am appalled at the carelessness with which we treat the environment — the Earth, God's gift to us. I find the arguments for continuing to manufacture destructive weapons of all types, with which to threaten and bully and kill people, morally repugnant. I find our acceptance of the status quo of gross commercial exploitation of less 'developed' and less industrialized nations arrogant and selfish. These issues do not form part of our confession, repentance and worship of God except peripherally, or for a few moments of intercessory prayer, or on some special occasion.

For me, feminist theology has confirmed that these concerns are part of my understanding of God, and my response to God, and that these responses are acceptable. I have an intellectual response to the abuse of the environment, which is that it does not make long-term economic sense, but I also have an emotional one, which is a desire to value and cherish an integrated life-system which is marvellous in its complexity. As for the arms trade, not only do I disagree with the logic for the continued trade in lethal weapons, but my gut reaction is one of repugnance for the callous disregard for human life that it represents.

The source of spiritual energy for me continues to be my personal relationship with God, which finds expression in prayer and reflection, and where possible in sharing with individuals and small groups the hopes and fears, the joys and the sadnesses, of coming to know God more fully.

It is traditional theology's lack of attention to women's experience (including the sensory and emotional experience) as having validity, that is part of what makes it unsatisfactory. Feminist theology attempts to redress this balance by exploring the wealth of women's experience of God outwith traditional understanding and practice, and asks whether we are prepared to discount the weight of evidence that God is much more than a single gender experience.

The new images of God and new ways of thinking of God which feminist theology has released have freed me to explore the presence of God from the inside out, instead of always trying to absorb God from the outside in. I have become aware of God within myself, as flame deep within my being. I imagine that as I travel in faith, the flame gradually illuminates more and more of my true self, revealing the smudged images and fudged truths which form me, to be transformed.

In my prayer I have reflected on powerful experiences of being held as a way of coming closer to God. One of my favourite experiences of being held is to drift weightless in the turquoise sea in a special place where I can also see the mountains towering brilliantly in the sunshine. I return often to this image of being cradled in the beauty of the natural world because it makes me feel completely connected to God's creation.

I have experienced the same sea in a powerful storm, in a wildly tossed boat, and felt the fragility of my life and the ultimate irrelevance of most of my concerns about ordering the chaos of the world. Sometimes I reflect on this image of vulnerability when I find the purpose of life evades me. The image reminds me that God is a power far beyond my limited understanding.

Another powerful image for me is of being clothed by God, as a loving person might wrap a garment round me. Sometimes I am clothed in a soft violet silk of consolation; sometimes in a light downy mantle of reassurance. It is a special feeling of being wrapped in cloth chosen uniquely for me, and I can feel the drape of silk on my shoulder or the cocoon of down as I pray.

These powerful images of cradling, vulnerability and clothing seem to me more feminine than masculine. I find they bring me nearer to an understanding of what it is to be loved by God than images of saving, rescuing or protecting with armour.

Of course there are dark times, when God seems remote, like a distant star in the black sky. Then I slide towards the abyss of unbelief. I feel acutely the absence of what is important to me—relatedness, integrity, affirmation. My sense of self diminishes and I feel valueless. My observation tells me that often men experience periods of unbelief when things they strive for in good faith — honesty, ethical dealings, fulfilling a vocation — seem to amount to nothing. For women, unbelief may go much deeper into a questioning of our very worth as human beings. For me, God always conjures footholds from nothing, offers the cliff-face against which I claw my way back, beckons me onwards across the wilderness, and keeps my innermost being alive by that flame within. It is in knowing God in the emotional and sensory part of me that helps me to keep faith with the belief that I am, as we all are, loved by God in my very self.

The outcome, or outcoming, since it is a continuous experience, is that I do not feel any longer defective, cringing from the image of a judgemental male God. My affective experience of God is not as a victorious king-like external being, but a sustainer of love and life, with both masculine and feminine aspects: power and patience, desire and tenderness, eagerness and calm, anger and sorrow. Many of my desires and fears have no place in traditional masculine theological explanations of how we are to know God. But I know them to be shared with other women, and to be valuable in the building up of our corporate understanding of what it is to be human and what it is to be loved by God.

In the end, we can only know what we know most profoundly by reflecting on our experience and using our imagination. Women have done theology in this way from time immemorial, but have not always proclaimed it so publicly. The upsurge of feminist theology has given many women confidence to speak about their understanding of God, and how they would like to express that both privately and publicly.

'The starting point for theology is our openness to that which we then name God. Theology is a second-order discipline. It is because our experience is what it is, that we undertake the task of theology.'[2]

Dreaming of Eden (i)

I watch them sometimes,
couples in their fifties.
They seem vital, purposeful,
still sexual,
not yet having reached the time of
metamorphosis
to ungendered old age
or long widowhood.

Staying on the straight road,
they have negotiated a way through
the irritable dislike of early familiarity,
the exhaustion of young parenthood,
the absence of feeling that frightened one day.
He didn't go off with another woman
to try it all again,
she resigned herself
to weaving her work round his.
They are a triumph of adaptability.

Now is the time of bringing in sheaves.
Children grown and gone,
more money, time
for travel,
good dinners,
old friends,
long-cherished plans,
pride in family
and the companionability of a lifetime.

It's not perfect.
So many losses.
But maybe
it's as good as it gets.

For the rest of your life: the deconstruction and reconstruction of marriage

Nearly thirty-four years of living together, in a marriage relationship that still seems to both of us to be working pretty well, all things considered, might be thought to be a fairly good background from which to say a few words on the subject of marriage today. But that's not how we see it. We view our thirty-odd years of marriage with a mixture of amazement and gratitude, certainly. But we also cannot fail to see the huge question marks that so many people — members of our own family as well as many of our friends —are raising about marriage. While there are certainly many, of both friends and family, whose marriages are things of strength and happiness, we also feel very deeply the pain and the hurt that so many people we love have experienced —are experiencing —both within marriage and within marriage breakdowns: both adults and children. Equally, we have come to value the nature of the relationships, and the giftedness of their lives together, of friends who have decided not to get married but who live together as partners, in either heterosexual or homosexual relationships.

To write about marriage is therefore not, for us, a very straightforward business! Things in this area of human relationship do not seem to us to be all that simple; and to write about marriage, as we do, from within the Christian tradition is, if anything, even harder. Our understanding of the Christian teaching about marriage — not to mention our understanding of our own marriage — is being constantly challenged by the experience of people very close to us; we are being driven, again and again, back to the basics of our belief. Perhaps, though, this is what Jesus meant when he said that the Spirit would lead us into the truth; not into some neat formula upon which we could rest and cease from thinking, but really 'back to basics', to coin a phrase!

Over forty years ago, the Iona Community published a pamphlet entitled *What is Christian Marriage?* It was written by Hugh Douglas, a Church of Scotland minister, and an Associate of the Community at the time. He had been one of George MacLeod's assistants in Govan, and went on to become Moderator of the General Assembly in 1970.

We thought we might use this pamphlet as a starting point. It has a rather special place in our family. The author, who died in 1986, was our respective father and father-in-law. His views on Christian marriage, not surprisingly, form part of the backdrop to our own thoughts on the subject. Not that we agree, or ever agreed, with them all!

Forty years on, the pamphlet actually reads very easily, and much in it still rings true today. There's nothing pious or pompous about it; it's very down-to-earth and basic. The author is quite clear that the increasing breakdown in marriages ('divorce five times as frequent as before the war') is a serious matter not just for the individuals involved, but also for the nation. He makes no claims for the guaranteed success of Christian as against secular marriages, but does set out, and argue very forcibly for his own view, that for marriage, the Christian faith still provides the surest foundation. Human beings, he argues, are both flesh and spirit; for two human beings to make a go of life together within the context of marriage, with all its joys and tensions, it requires full recognition to be given to both parts of our natures. In a section entitled 'The Transforming Spirit', he puts forward the traditional Christian view, that sees God, in Christ, showing us how to do this; and invites us to recognize therefore the value of faith in Christ as a central plank in any marriage platform. The Christian understanding of love, as expounded by St Paul in 1 Corinthians 13, applies, he suggests, as much within the marriage relationship as within any; which is no doubt why, even today, it is still one of the favourite readings in a Christian wedding ceremony.

The pamphlet is not, and never sought to be, an exhaustive treatment of marriage. And in both its style and content, it reflects a settled and uncomplicated view of Christian marriage and human relationships which really wouldn't speak to a lot of couples in today's much more confusing world. Nevertheless, we would argue that its main propositions remain as valid today, from a Christian point of view, as they were four decades ago. We see our own marriage, very largely, within the same context still. At the same time, it is glaringly obvious that marriage today is under a huge strain. Marriage Counselling Scotland counselled 500 couples in Glasgow alone in 1996; double the number they saw a few years ago. One-third of the total number of couples seen by MCS aren't actually married; in 1997, it is expected that 6000 couples in Scotland will divorce. Recent research suggests that we are seeing a significant number of people, particularly women, who now choose quite deliberately to live on their own — and are free, economically as well as emotionally, to do so. A recent Social Trends report states that married-couple households, seventy-one per cent of the total twenty-five years ago, are already down to fifty per cent of all homes, and look set to drop to forty-two per cent by 2016. We are by no means unique in the number of friends we have, of our own age and younger, whose marriages have ended in divorce or separation; and we know a number of couples, heterosexual and homosexual, who choose to seek a stable relationship outside marriage.

What has happened to marriage?

So what has happened to marriage over these four decades in Britain? And, perhaps more pertinently for the purposes of this book, what are Christians to do about it? A quotation from the expanded *Diary of Anne Frank* presents the challenge in movingly simple terms.

> I believe love is something that really can't be put into words. Love is understanding someone, caring for someone, sharing their ups and downs. And in the long run, that also means physical love, you have shared something, given something away, and received something, no matter whether you are married or unmarried, or whether you are with child or not. It doesn't matter in the least if you have lost your honour, as long as you know that someone will stand by you, will understand you for the rest of your life, someone you won't have to share with anyone else.[1]

We want to be as upfront as we can about our own marriage. And the basis upon which we believe it rests. Marriage, as we understood it in the 1960s, and as we still understand it today, is for life. It is the best setting within which to share the whole of life, flesh and spirit, with another human being. It is the strongest foundation for coping with the stresses and strains of living in today's, or any day's, world. It is the best relationship within which to have and bring up children, and it works best if it is based on the Christian faith in God as love, as expressed in the life of Jesus and in the insights of Scripture and the Christian tradition at its highest.

These, we realize, are large claims. And we would not for one minute offer our marriage as a flawless example of them in practice! We don't know any marriage that could. In making them, however, we want to do more than simply state that they are the view on which our marriage is based. For this view obviously did not descend, complete and unabridged, from heaven by way of the Christian church, or even an Iona Community pamphlet. What was the social and cultural infrastructure on which it stood?

There seem to us to be three main elements. Family life, on the whole, was pretty stable in middle-class Britain when we were growing up in the late 1940s and 1950s. Issues of sexual orientation, and the notion of 'being in a relationship' were rarely discussed, and divorce, while certainly on the increase, was relatively rare. Marriage, as a natural development of life in your early twenties, was something you expected to enter, just as you took it for granted that you would, at roughly the same time or perhaps a bit earlier, get a job which you could expect to last for life. These expectations were based on the fact — or at least, we assumed it to be a fact — of a stable society within which we would go on living; the Welfare State, economic growth, peace (or at least the absence of hot war in Europe), low unemployment, rising living standards, and a population which would continue to be healthy and relatively wealthy, if not necessarily especially wise.

Not surprisingly, therefore, the Christian view of marriage that we inherited was not difficult to fit comfortably onto this infrastructure. To say this is not to make the Christian view of marriage simply into something relative to a particular social climate. Rather is it to recognize what Christian ethical and moral teaching has always recognized; that particular social and cultural conditions always affect the way in which Christians live out their faith. And it raises, for us, what is perhaps the most urgent question around marriage today, at least for followers of the Christian faith. How do we uphold the best in the Christian view of marriage, in a social and cultural climate hugely different, and much less friendly, than that of forty and fifty years ago?

Not that the changes over this period have all been for the worse. We would argue that some of them have been. Whatever Mrs Thatcher may have meant by her now notorious statement about there being 'no such thing as society' she was surely articulating not only something that she herself believed and helped to promote, but also something which was believed by a very large number of people in this country. Alongside the growing 'me first' generation, there has grown up an increasing feeling that 'what I want, I have a right to have, and have it now'; that 'I can do what

I like with my life, with my body, with my money'; that, 'life's too short, and if other folk get hurt, too bad'. The so-called 'sexual revolution' has brought a number of benefits, not least to women; the downside, it could be argued, has been the isolating of sex, from the rest of life, and the marketing of sex as something good and whole in itself; a concept as ridiculous, when you think about it, as suggesting the same about marketing blinking, or breathing, or defecating!

But there have been changes for the better, too. The growing self-awareness and confidence of women has led, at least in part, to an increasing recognition of the importance of things like sensitivity, gentleness, emotion and loyalty in relationships. The trend to more honesty and less formality in relationships has helped to undermine a fair bit of hypocrisy and sham in many marriages; not always, it has to be said, without a cost, but perhaps at a cost more willingly paid in the long run. The growth in both sophistication and availability of effective contraceptive methods of birth control has facilitated responsible family planning in a way earlier generations could not have imagined; although this has clearly contributed to the dangerous trend of isolating the sexual act from the rest of a relationship, and the growing number of pregnancies among school pupils raises serious questions about sex and relationship education in the teenage years, and the seeming lack of purpose particularly in the lives of so many young girls.

Then there is what is known as 'the declining influence of the church'. In a discussion about marriage and the Christian position in relation to it, this phrase, we feel, needs a bit of expansion.

Clearly it is necessary to differentiate in the first place between 'church weddings' and 'Christian marriage'. Sometimes, but probably only in a minority of cases, the two phrases relate to the same reality. Fewer and fewer couples are going to church to get married now. And we don't know the number of couples who decide to dispense with any form of marriage, religious or civil.

The challenge to the church

On that basis, it can be argued that the influence of the church on marriage is certainly in decline. We would want to qualify that bald statement, however, with three comments. One, obviously, is that the influence of the church on the whole of life in Britain today is in decline; young people whose lives have hardly been touched by the church in any meaningful way during childhood and youth are unlikely, of themselves, to turn to the church if and when they decide to get married. But — our second thought — if they do, then they present, whether they know it or not, (and quite often they do) a huge challenge to the church. How can the fundamentals of the Christian faith, as they relate to marriage in today's world, be shared and be sustained, with and for people for whom the institutional church plays at best a minimal part in their lives? A third thought, then, is this. What is God trying to tell us —all of us, both within the church and outside it —through the struggles, successes and failures of the marriages that have broken down, and of the relationships into which more and more people are entering these days, which are not encompassed within the Christian marriage covenant? And are we willing to listen — and to learn?

Here, we want to reclaim the word 'relationship'. Today, it is mainly used to refer to the lifestyle of a couple who are living together *outside* marriage, in that context, it has arguably been the core word around which a lot of hard, valuable work has been done on how two human beings can get on together. We think of friends and family members who have contributed their fair share of hard-won experience to this area of human experience. In their struggles (mainly, it has to be said, either outwith marriage or in the midst of marital breakdown) they have often offered us quite new insights into the meaning of words like honesty, truth, loyalty, acceptance, sensitivity and love — whose meaning has become lost or buried for many under layers of what has too often seemed to be simply religious jargon or empty formulae.

The challenge to the church here we see as finding a way to honour these struggles towards deep relationships within marriage. The church has the same problem here as it does with the process of becoming a church member. Too often, the impression is given that once you have had the knot tied by a priest or minister, that's the end of the process; whereas it is, of course, only the beginning.

Certainly there are some signs that the church is recognizing the need to support and encourage the growth and struggle of relationships within marriage; meetings for couples are arranged, conferences happen, counselling is offered. What we do not know of — maybe it is happening somewhere — are opportunities being offered where married couples, couples in other sorts of relationships (including homosexual ones) and single people can work together both at valuing what is good in their different sorts of relationships, and also at exploring the difficulties and problems that they each face, *without* the judgementalism that so often emanates from the church about relationships other than married ones.

This, of course, brings us back to the question of why the church is so judgemental about these other sorts of relationships; and deeper still, it takes us to the question, what *is* the fundamental reality of relationship which Christians want to offer to the world? This is the challenge that is posed by the people who come, usually from a secular background, and often already living together, to seek a church wedding. Only a gospel response will do.

A starting point here surely has to be the willingness to take seriously the previous experience of the people who come. Whether they have lived together, or have had other partners before their present one, is not a matter for judgement or for condemnation; indeed, is not at this point a matter for comment at all. It is a matter of fact, to be acknowledged and taken seriously, for it will have been a serious matter for them, and will have helped to form their view of life, whatever ideas the church, officially, may have of what that view *ought* to be.

Where the conversation can go next, is, perhaps surprisingly, to the person of Jesus. But people expect the church, after all, to speak about Jesus; who he is and what it is about him that keeps on drawing people to him still, it usually doesn't take too long to elicit from people, even people for whom Christian things are no more than a memory of Sunday School, or boring assemblies at day school, or perhaps simply a couple of 'Bible movies' caught over Christmas on television, that the central and memorable thing about Jesus is what he said, and more importantly what he *did* about love. This can be illustrated in many ways; the story of Jesus and the woman taken in adultery (John 8:1-11); the parable of the Prodigal Son (Luke 15:11-32); and the account of the death of Jesus (Mark 15 is perhaps the most appropriate); they all, in different ways, ring bells for people. To go on from there to look at the insights of Paul about the nature of love, 'love is patient and kind; it is not jealous or conceited or proud; love is not ill-mannered or selfish or irritable; love does not keep a record of wrongs; love is not happy with evil, but is happy with the truth. Love never gives up; and its faith, hope and patience never fail', *(1 Corinthians 13:4-7)* is usually to make a lot of sense to people. Not only are they very well aware that love is at the heart of any relationship that is going to work, including marriage; they also recognize (usually with a few wry smiles at their own failure to live up to his high standard!) the reality of what Paul is talking about. They have been there.

Where they will also, in most cases, have been, is to the place where that sort of love *hurts*. It's important, surely, to get to this place fairly early on. *Cheap* love is simply not worth talking about. Sadly, it seems to be the case that a lot of people think that is what Christian marriage is about. It's not. To focus on what it cost Jesus to love like that; if possible, to get even deeper and talk about what it cost God to love like that; is to move with people to the place where there is no avoiding the reality of relationships. It's also to move there very firmly within the core Christian tradition.

Of course, the Christian tradition also speaks of the loving that *heals*. This again rings bells with people in most cases; this will probably already have been their experience, either in their present relationship, or in an earlier one, for example, as a child in a family. And all of this can fairly easily be related to the Christian marriage service, with its celebration of the loving nature of God in Christ, and the prayers for the couple, that the God who is love will continue to be part of their relationship for the rest of their lives.

What needs to happen after the wedding service is, if anything, the greater challenge. We've already said that this is only the beginning of the relationship. We've already noted some of the pressures that will inevitably bear down on virtually every marriage today. Add to these pressures parenting, employment problems, financial constraints, perhaps health worries, the care of elderly relatives and it becomes very clear that the love that both hurts and heals is going to have to work overtime if the relationship is going to survive. Can the church offer the sort of community of honesty and openness within which these often confusing, at times conflicting pressures can be shared and dealt with, without losing sight of the basics of Christian belief?

To answer that, it would probably be best to find ways of listening to Christian people who have been there themselves. Some of them will be single, some celibate. Some of them will be married. Some will have been married, and will have been through the ending of their marriage, and perhaps the beginning of another one. Some will not have been married at all, but will have lived with a partner, or perhaps a series of partners. Some of the relationships will have been heterosexual, some homosexual. In all of them there will have been signs of the love that hurts and the love that heals. To listen to what they have to say; to give them permission to say it without judging or condemning; to offer a community of love within which to grow as human beings amidst all the complexities of life; from such a community, might not a worthwhile word go out to a world increasingly desperate both for community and for love? And if we remember that the biblical word for 'salvation' comes from a word whose basic meaning is about giving people space, then this message would seem, would it not, to be in tune with the Jesus who said, 'I came not to judge the world but to save it'? *(John 12:47)*

Blooming women

At the garden's edge
I see the waiting women
of all time.

From the margin of history
they put the buds
of their silence
into my hands
outstretched from the future.

And the flowers that open
are vibrant and outrageous
blooming with all the colours
of a new centre of being
which is my body
and my surprise.

Celibacy: a subversive proclamation of Christian freedom, or sexual repression

Reflecting on celibacy puts me in mind of a time in my life in my early thirties when I was passionately in love. I was then a member of a religious order where I made an annual vowed commitment which included celibacy. Being in love disturbed that commitment and put me in touch with all the range of feelings between agony and ecstasy. It involved me at the same time in a searing soul-search of my initial reasons for choosing celibacy. The slow painful outcome was a deeper sense that married love was not my gift and life went on.

A second set of questions were revealed through the soul search about the value of marriage compared to celibacy. Could it be that the best way to learn about who God is and what God is like is through a committed one-to-one sexual relationship? If physical sexual expression is a spiritual experience of ecstasy and abandonment why hasn't the church been more positive in the value it places on sexuality? Why do some people, in the name of gospel values, choose to deny or refrain from this wholesome experience? While such questions are valid in their own right, they also reveal the influence of a hierarchical value system which sought to place celibacy above marriage.

In the following reflections I will look at what I think celibacy is. I will examine the difference between celibacy as rule and celibacy as gift, including the place of aloneness and friendship in the context of celibacy. I will explore women's cultural conditioning and feminism in relation to celibacy, and will conclude with some questions and reflections.

Celibacy as a life choice

As a way of life within the Christian tradition celibacy may date back to Jesus the itinerant preacher who turned the values of stability and family life on their head in favour of freedom, autonomy and a community of co-equal disciples. Celibacy is choosing to live as a sexual being in a way that precludes a committed sexual relationship which is genitally active. The reasons people choose celibacy are varied: some wish to make a single-minded commitment to the person of Jesus Christ; some feel called to a lifestyle which requires one to be celibate, for example, priesthood in the Roman Catholic church or membership of a canonical religious order; some wish to give themselves totally to one thing, such as scholarship, missionary work, art, music; some have had few opportunities to meet and mix with their contemporaries, perhaps due to family commitments; some have had traumatic childhood experiences resulting in a fear of intimate relationships; the model of life experienced by some in their childhood can be a challenge to seek an alternative way of life. Celibacy then is an inclusive term covering the many and varied states of singleness where people find themselves, from living in community to living alone.

The element of choice is as significant a component for celibacy as it is for marriage. Any sense of it being imposed, unwelcome or circumstantial makes it a negative rather than a positive life choice. This is not to undervalue or exclude any person's experience. Witness the example of women who lost lovers in the war and who wanted to be faithful to their memory or who met no-one who could replace that memory. Numbers of these women devoted their lives in a single-minded way to teaching, nursing or other such careers.

The norm for all adult relationships in our patriarchal society is the couple. Celibates are required to re-interpret this norm by affirming the uniqueness, completeness, integrity and identity of the individual. This is especially important for women who frequently take their identity and their power from partners and sometimes from their children, and this can result in an undeveloped sense of their own identity.

Celibacy as rule or as gift

Western culture and history is emerging from generations, even centuries of sexual repression. Every revolution is disturbing and brings both positive and negative facets to the surface. Arising from this sexual revolution is the challenge to re-examine attitudes and hangups which hide the value of sex as a creative energy and a gift to be celebrated. On the other hand, there is the less positive tendency to measure much of life in a sexual way — to make an idol of such a gift by exploiting it as a marketing tool. Most of the advertising on our television screens is subliminal, containing covert sexual imagery. There are in society double standards in the way sexual norms are applied differently to women from those applied to men. Confusion exists around the relationship between sex and power, all indicating that society is still in the throes of the sexual revolution.

Celibacy has not remained immune from this upheaval, both for those seeking to live this lifestyle and those looking on from outside. The rule of celibacy creates problems today because of its restrictive focus. In the context of priesthood in the Roman Catholic church, celibacy is mandatory — it is a means to priesthood for men who will not be accepted into priesthood without agreeing to abide by the rule of celibacy. The call to priesthood is synonymous with the call to celibacy. Put the other way the rules are different — one can be a celibate without being a priest. While many priests may feel called and deeply committed to celibacy, the linking of priesthood with celibacy means that the authenticity of celibacy as a way of life in its own right is diminished.

While acknowledging that tying priesthood to celibacy with a rule is a weakness, this is not in my view the cause of sexual abuse by members of the clergy. Society with its obsession with sex would have us believe otherwise. Every denomination is burdened with members of the clergy who abuse their positions of trust by initiating sexual relationships with members of their parish, employees or people in vulnerable situations. Society responds differently when such abuse is committed by celibate male clergy within the Roman Catholic church, blaming the rule of celibacy regardless of the number of women exploited. Ethical and moral questions raised by such behaviour are rarely examined either by the offending individual, the church hierarchies or society in general. It is often left to the victims and survivors to struggle alone with these ethical issues while society prefers to blame celibacy rather than take on the challenge of examining how power is abused in such relationships.

Celibacy as gift and as call has a longer Christian history than the rule of celibacy. This consecrated celibacy as a charism or gift from God symbolizes something of the wholeness of God and the sufficiency in the relationship between the individual and God. For some, the gift of celibacy is without a sacrificial element because there is a sense that marriage is just not right for them, while for others there is a 'giving up' aspect within the gift of celibacy.

It is the freeing nature of celibacy that is its creative force — its gift. A gift holds potential related to need in each generation. The gift of celibacy in today's world symbolizes authenticity — the treasured gift of one's own uniqueness offered for an ideal, for the person of Jesus Christ, for kingdom values of justice and love. It also symbolizes the need in our society for just relationships between women and men as well as being a reminder of the aloneness which is the part of each one's life.

Celibacy and aloneness

Learning to accept aloneness is part of our journey towards maturity. This is as true for couples as it is for those who are single. Mostly, human beings want to avoid confronting aloneness. We crowd our lives with distractions, busyness, consumerism and compulsions in order to avoid making that inward journey to the place where each of us has to stand alone with our poverty as well as our wealth. Some space for solitude is necessary for this inward journey and celibacy has the potential and the capacity for such space — an emptiness that enables the individual to be more in tune with the divine within. Celibacy then is a nurturing ground for solitude, for aloneness and for communion with God.

Friendship within celibacy

As with so much of the spiritual life there is a paradox too within celibacy. Aloneness and solitude on the one hand, and on the other loving availability. As sexual beings all our relationships have a sexual dimension. We relate through our bodies and we relate through our gender. We notice maleness and femaleness all the time. Availability brings us into contact with people, and relationships are formed. There is every possibility that those with a commitment to celibacy will meet and be in relationship with someone who could potentially be a life partner. Such mutual friendship enhances psychological and emotional health, creates balance in one's life and energizes one's ministry.

Such relationships are more likely to thrive if they are built on some secure foundations. A clear commitment to celibacy as well as a commitment to strategies and safeguards which avoid compromise in one's commitment will allow for a healthy and open friendship within the context of celibacy. Warning signs of exclusivity, secrecy, dishonesty and disregard for sexual boundaries should alert the committed celibate to the need for reflection with the help of a trusted counsellor of colleague.

Friendship within the context of committed celibacy must be seen in the light of one great love that enhances every other love.

Some historical trends

While this essay makes no claim to be a historical treatise, there are some interesting strands to note from history. A monastic lifestyle that included a commitment to celibacy has been part of Christianity from as early as the fifth century. A number of such monasteries and orders came into being as protest movements against the established status quo. They were almost all radical in their foundation. In Europe during the twelfth century, lay women and lay men within the church began to seek an alternative to monastic enclosure. Lay fraternities attached to the Franciscans and the Dominicans came to birth and at the same time lay groups of women known as the 'Beguines' came into being in the Low Countries.

The Beguines are particularly interesting because they manifested different trends from other lay fraternities. Membership was female only and included both women living alone and women in community. They never became a cohesive group with a named leader or an organized structure. They promised to remain chaste while living as beguines but they were free to marry or to join an established religious order. What united this disparate group of individuals was a desire to lead a committed Christian life together with other women, without the constraints imposed by marriage or enclosure.

The Beguines were popular and influential in their time and could probably be described as the first European women's movement. Their orientation was towards the poor and the sick and they earned their living by manual work. They avoided institutionalization while reaping the benefits of community living. As an independent community of women they posed a challenge to society's definition of women's roles. The power to avoid traditional stereotyping, to discover their own potential and to compose and control their own institutions, however culturally conditioned and vulnerable these attempts may have been, represent the great strength and originality of the beguine movement.

Celibacy and feminism

Looking specifically at the role of women in society, how does celibacy and feminism co-relate? The reclaiming of women's bodies and women's sexuality has been part of the feminist agenda in the way it has highlighted the male colonization of female sexuality and the dualism within the Christian tradition about the bodily and the spiritual. Feminism has also uncovered the way culture has stereotyped women in a way that has benefited men. Such stereotyping has included the role of passive and dependent wife and homemaker, and has meant greater vulnerability to domestic abuse and violence for women. Feminism has made inroads into every discipline and every institution, uncovering similar patterns everywhere in relationships between women and men.

Just as the Beguines revealed a different expression of a celibate lifestyle, so the examination of women's history shows that most women who made a significant contribution to pre-reformation culture were either nuns or women living in celibacy within or after marriage. Celibacy provided women with freedom and opportunities that were denied to them in marriage. Opting for celibacy required considerable courage in a patriarchal marriage-centred culture.

One of today's tensions surround the place institutions hold and how we relate to them. Religious orders are no exception. In many cases, their founding radical edge has disappeared and because of the wider choices available today such communities are no longer the sole providers of an alternative lifestyle. One outcome may be that the church will have less hold and control of celibacy.

The church as a whole has been too narrow in its definitions of lifestyle. Marriage is the only real option within most denominations. The Roman Catholic church caters for a second category, namely, those committed either to consecrated celibacy or bound by the rule of celibacy. These are under the church's jurisdiction as either ordained priests, members of religious orders, or as individuals who vow celibacy under the jurisdiction of their bishop and work within the context of a diocese. Can the church widen its interest in celibacy beyond those who are under its jurisdiction? Will it find a language that speaks to the many committed and devoted Christians who are celibate either by choice or through circumstances, and affirm singleness as an authentic and positive lifestyle.

A challenge and a sign

Consecrated celibacy within the Christian tradition has been a liberating energy for many who willingly gave their whole lives to God. However, the church must address the restrictive nature of mandatory celibacy which potentially undervalues the gift of celibacy. It is as sexual beings that celibacy is embraced and lived out as a symbol of the wholeness in God. It is a statement on the need for just relationships between women and men. Today especially it offers a challenge to the church to surrender ownership of this gift and to find a new and inclusive language to redefine its meaning and its value. It offers a challenge to today's sex-obsessed world seeking to be for the young a countersign to peer pressure, as well as being a radical alternative for many who are aware of the risk of AIDS. It still holds its place as a subversive sign for women, refusing to have them cast in stereotypical roles and defined by reproductive gifts alone.

Dreaming of Eden (ii)

no gays
(Adam and Adam!)

no-one past childbearing age
or under the age of consent

nobody fat
(not naked!)

no-one with parents
(conflict of loyalties)
and no siblings
competing for attention

no-one with diseases

no-one who is not a virgin

and definitely
no-one curious

no wonder there were only two of them

The cost of denial

AIDS is nothing. Like evil in scholastic definition it lacks the dignity and status of being. The acquired immune deficiency syndrome manifests itself not as an entity, but as the collapse of the body's defences, an emptying out of its vigour and the yielding of its territory to cancers, fungal infections, pneumonias. With its immune system compromised the body succumbs to a kind of physical *privatio boni*. HIV infection is known by its terrible fruits; the wasting and collapsing of which AIDS is the final state.

Its presence among us has caused a general examination of our practices. Are our sexual habits 'safe'? How much do our children know and understand about relationships, about sexuality? In today's plural society what do we ourselves believe about these matters? What makes people inject drugs? At the onset of the pandemic, medics, dentists, nurses all at once began to adhere to strict codes of sterile practice which they should have been adhering to already; suddenly that negligible risk of cross-infection could result in fatalities. The virus acted like a tracer element in systems larger than the human body, highlighting weaknesses and *lacunae* in the law, in education, in insurance policies, in social welfare, in medical and nursing practice, in spirituality and in the response of the Christian churches.

For like the rest of human society, the church is now HIV positive. The Body of Christ has HIV infection, and like any carrier of the virus it would do well to examine its ways. For an individual, a positive diagnosis is likely to be terrifying. But after the initial confusion, fear and denial there may come a reassessment of priorities, of the meaning of life. People who are HIV positive are encouraged to take responsibility for the years or months that remain and to live their lives to the full. If they are wise they begin to care for themselves, improve their diet, exercise, think positively, strive to stay well. Existential and spiritual questions arise and can no longer be shelved till later. There may *be* no 'later'.

We are the Body of Christ, and individually limbs and organs of it. How is our immune system? What of our general health? What weaknesses does HIV expose in our midst? What is the challenge of AIDS to the churches?

When we were first infected by the virus our initial response was admirable, but familiar and habitual. We initiated schemes of support and care for infected individuals. The church has a long and noble history of caring for the poor and the sick, and we did not all hold back. Many have shown a loving care which is in the spirit of Christ.

And yet, without wishing in the least to denigrate the magnificent caring response that many individuals and groups have adopted, I sometimes suspect that it enables the rest of us to avoid deeper, more searching issues that the virus poses to us. The caring response leaves us, in a sense, off the hook. We are the strong nurturing the weak, the 'haves' being charitable to the 'have-nots', the healthy exercising compassion to the sick. But are we ourselves entirely healthy? Our compassionate stance can shield us from the question. I am reminded of the contrast between Mother Teresa, everyone's favourite saint, who devotes herself tirelessly to the welfare of the dying, 'tending the wounds of Christ', but asks no questions of the system that lets them die in the gutter; and on the other hand, Dom Helder Camara, who remarked, 'When I give bread to the poor, people call me a saint. If I ask why the poor have no bread they call me a communist.'[1] To ask questions other than how best to care is to risk a sharp drop in popularity.

I have represented the Episcopal church over the last two years in the Strathclyde Interchurch AIDS Project, and it has largely been in that context that I have found my own attitudes and those of the church sharply scrutinized and questioned. I want to address two related areas of weakness for us; our acceptance of homosexual people and the sexuality of our clergy.

Taking funerals for those who have died of AIDS we may find ourselves comforting a grieving partner of the same sex. Unless we are extraordinarily heartless we will be gentle, recognize the love that was there, mention the name of the partner in our prayers.

What on earth is it about the fact of death that suddenly makes it possible publicly to acknowledge a gay partnership? Where were we when the couple were falling in love, exploring the risks of commitment? Did we support them in their life together, encourage fidelity, offer them a place in our community? It seems that recognition can only be accorded when one partner is lying in his coffin. Richard Holloway remarks in *Anger, Sex, Doubt and Death* that we are better at coping with the quiet problems of dying than with the noisy problems of living.

One of the most depressing elements of our failure here is that so many of the clergy are themselves homosexual. If we were removed from office the church would grind to a halt (although my respect for the laity makes me doubt if our deposition would be such a disaster after all ...). The matter is known about but not often aired in a healthy fashion. Rather it breaks surface every now and then in a flurry of tabloid headlines. The sexual fantasies of a senior priest are offered to readers of *The Sunday Sport* and he departs for a discreet chaplaincy somewhere off the beaten track; an ex-Franciscan is murdered by a pick-up; a parish priest is found to have been conducting a long affair with a married minister. And there are all those too sad, too boring or too careful to hit the headlines. More often poor old so-and-so with a congregation down to single figures and a cupboard full of empty bottles (but one bleary eye open for his fanciable milkman) just disappears one day to a muted murmur of episcopal euphemisms.

Recently I attended a regional council meeting in our diocese at which a debate took place concerning the ordination of women to the priesthood. One speaker against the motion declared that, in her opinion, female feminist clergy would be a terrible imposition but preferable to a homosexual priest. What was the image in her mind? What do we 'model' for our congregations? Alas, too often, duplicity, hypocrisy, the pathological defence of splitting. Many gay clergy have been used to lying for years; we have lied to ourselves, our families, our churches and our God, and the mask of the parsonical celibate that we wear in church is a lie. As role models for young gay people in our congregations we characteristically demonstrate highly developed skills in how to avoid self knowledge and how to lead a double life. Rarely does a priest (even a straight one!) celebrate his God-given sexuality, talk of it with joy, joke about it, relate it to prayer and the love of God. Many gay clergy wear a mask of denial an inch thick, and, like St Peter, cursing and swearing by his third denial of Christ, they have virtually come to believe their own lie.

All this is cloaked, of course, in a 'decent reticence', the 'right to a private life', 'professionalism', and talk of the undesirability of scandalizing the faithful. And so the old lie goes on. Meanwhile, the people of God do not meet their pastor. They meet an image of him; his true reality is well hidden and often tragically unintegrated. Let no one doubt the scale of the problem; Malcolm Johnson, interviewed in *The Guardian* in November 1992 observed:

I run a support group for 450 gay priests. By and large most live a hidden life. They are fearful to talk about the most meaningful part of their life, their sexuality. However, very few are celibate. They would probably like to be thought celibate, and their congregations would like to think they are celibate, but I can assure you that the majority are not and therefore there is a lack of integrity within our ranks.

But given the respectable attitudes of the people of God, how is honesty possible? The corruption is fed by a vicious circle: the homophobic atmosphere of the church and society makes openness costly and difficult, and many men and women as a result repress the knowledge of their own sexual identities. Repressed and unintegrated sexuality emerges bizarrely, and the fear and suspicion that this generates adds to the atmosphere of disapproval. How on earth does a gay priest ever manage to make sexuality a normal, healthy part of his life (that is, integrate it) in an environment where he risks losing his license if he enters a stable gay relationship? And how on earth does a congregation come to love a furtive gay priest whose heart they can never get near enough to read? Kenneth Leech puts it like this:

In many ways, however, the church is still caught in the position which prevailed in society as a whole before the reforming legislation and the emergence of the gay liberation movement. Hence the terrible atmosphere of dishonesty and doublespeak which makes serious discussion of this issue virtually impossible in many church circles. Hence too the practical consequences of this atmosphere, described so well by John Fortunato:

'Lonely, isolated gay priests in remote backwaters quietly drinking themselves to death. Gay ministers trying to pastor — by definition, an intimate undertaking — but having to leave an enormous piece of their personhood outside the pastoral relationship. Quietly seething congregations who must deal with an evasive gay father who is present but never really present. Gay priests or ministers who vote at church conventions or synods or conferences for the oppression of gay people in order to protect their reputations. There are literally thousands of clergy in such situations in the church today leading schizophrenic anxious lives. If only we could lift up their wholeness, how much blessing the church would know once again.'[2]

Rowan Williams makes a similar point when he says that: 'it is becoming harder all the time for a gay person to be *honest* in the church. We have helped to build a climate in which concealment is rewarded — while at the same time conniving in the hysteria of the gutter press, and effectively giving into their hands as victims all those who do not manage successful concealment.'[3]

Now, it is notoriously misleading to confuse homosexuality with paedophilia. Self-affirming gay people are probably even less likely to offend in this area than heterosexuals, but the abuse of children and vulnerable adults in pastoral situations is not helped by the closeted and unhealthy sexual environment in which we live. Inadequate sexual integration is the key factor again. If for religious and social reasons sexuality has become the Dangerous Enemy Within, you keep it behind bars. It is an alienated and angry force, not a friend, and there is no proper field for its expression. If you have never developed confidence in yourself as a sexual being in relationships of equality, a child is less threatening, an easier option. They can be seduced, dominated, silenced. Similarly, the priest may have no confidence in himself as a sexual man, but find he is in a powerful and intimate position as a pastor. The collar can bring distinct advantages here, and it may even be possible to convince yourself that what is going on is not sexual but spiritual! It is instructive to compare the average gay pub or singles bar (those dens of iniquity and breeding grounds of HIV) with what goes on in the privacy of many a priest's study. As John Rutter's book *Sex in the Forbidden Zone* makes plain, the abuse of women and vulnerable men by members of the caring professions is unbelievably widespread — and universally denied. But in the pubs sexuality is open, acknowledged, adult. Men and women meet on an equal footing and have to affirm themselves and ask directly for what they want. A healthier situation, surely, for all its promiscuity.

This then is the world that AIDS has come to challenge, and I submit that it is not a healthy one.

Yet it is at the heart of every Christian to reach out in loving acceptance to the marginalized. In loving the least of Christ's brothers and sisters we love him, and if we say we love him while despising his and our brother or sister, we are liars. How may we express love?

I suggest that some open discussion of the homosexual issue should take place in the Episcopal church. The fear and closeted furtiveness of gay clergy and laity is fed at the moment by ignorance, prejudice and the strange fantasies of many uninformed church people. As a community we are not a safe or an honest place. Yet there are many gay men and lesbian women longing for recognition, love, acceptance, who should be among us already. We can be a place of healing if we will but dispel the darkness from our hearts.

No fear in love

There were four of them, two each for my mother and me, and she declared as we peeled and munched that she had never seen pomegranates so large, so sweet, so juicy.

'And at this time of year! Where on earth did you get them?'

I had never eaten a pomegranate before, and I had not recognized these funny onion-shaped things. In the Glasgow of the 1970s pomegranates were about as common as silver nutmegs and golden pears. But I had heard of them, and there clung to the word an odour of sanctity and sublimated sex, something biblical ...

> As a piece of pomegranate are thy temples
> Behind thy veil

My Plymouth Brethren mind supplied the reference. Song of Songs. Him talking about her. Sounds quite sexy, but really means Jesus and the church, i.e., miles up in the air, lots of purity, white lights and low temperatures.

> 'From a guy at university. His English was not very good, and I was able to help him with something. He gave me these as a thank-you present ...'

And he did too. His English was rudimentary but had been sufficient to the occasion. Which of us had helped the other is perhaps more debatable. I had been to a meeting of the Christian Union that night; we were reading through Joshua and listening for what God was saying to us in the pages of the Word. Rahab the Harlot had hidden the Israelite spies and had been spared during the sack of Jericho. I liked the story but wondered that the immorality of Rahab's profession was not more of a problem; and why had they gone there in the first place? 'Go and see the land, even Jericho, commands Joshua, son of Nun,' *(Joshua 2:1)* and the two spies head straight for the red-light district.

But then is this not a lesson to us that the gospel has to be preached in the darkest places first? Given the University to convert, should we not begin with the department of mechanical engineering, or even the

Beer bar? Together we transmuted all that glorious barbarous stuff into a message of encouragement to us to renew our outreach to the halls of residence; all the magic of the Old Testament, standing waters, priests and trumpets, city walls, ambushes, mass slaughter and great dramatic prayers with clothes rent and prostrate before the ark! What is God saying to us, we asked earnestly. Ah yes, as the Lord heard the prayer of Joshua, he would hear ours for the conversion of our non-Christian friends. Joshua had spent all day praying; how long did we spend? Ai had fallen, would not the university — or at least the first spoils the department of nursing studies, a bastion known already to be weakened by the presence within it of so many of the Lord's people?

It was after that meeting that I met my 'stranger in the Land' whose English was not very good and who needed my help. I was in my early twenties and pious to a degree and unlike Rahab I was a virgin. It had long been clear to me that I was homosexual in orientation and indeed rather unambivalently so. The female form, as I had already gloomily concluded registered zero on the Richter scale, but the sight, sound or even idea of men, the wilder the better, could make the earth move at the most inconvenient times and in the wrong company. And somehow I was always at my worst for a few hours after the Wednesday night Christian Union meeting.

What can I say about him? I do not even remember his name. He had the platform shoes and embroidered jeans jacket that we wore in those days, and we made love in his frowsy little bedsit. But when I left that night I was full of joy. Someone had touched with interest, excitement, my scrawny little body, and I had come to life. I ran to catch the bus home, clutching his parting gift, grinning ecstatically, thinking, I'm alive, I'm real, I'm beautiful, I can do it, I am like other people. On the bus, I found myself alone upstairs and sang aloud. As a youth of extreme piety all the music I knew really well was hymns; 'Jesus saves!' I carolled, 'Will your anchor hold in the storms of life?' My body felt new born, light, I was floating, laughing, silly.

Sodom and Gomorrah, began the God of Joshua in a distant rumble, but I did not care. If Jesus wanted me for a sunbeam one look at my face would have convinced him that I was shining bright enough.

'Delicious,' reiterated my mother gathering up a few little pinkish globules that had fallen off her plate. 'It's a shame for these lads from fallen parts struggling with their English. I'm glad you were able to help him.'

But the God of Joshua and I had unfinished business. That night as the uproar in my hormones settled down a little I remembered that in a few days time I had to conduct a Bible study (my first as leader!) and already that night I should pray through my list of non-Christians.

The chaplains were my particular burden; that they might be converted and become real Christians. Now these were the days before the Alpha course and Nicky Gumbel had not yet been saved, but my generation too had its shining ones, and their teaching all concurred, unconfessed sin meant God would not answer your prayers and in whatever you did you would not prosper. However long your list of non-Christians, and however fervently you prayed it, the heavens would be as brass if there was some sin you had not laid before the mercy-seat. And the Bible study would not prosper. I might prepare carefully, but the words would carry no conviction; and that was judgement. That was God saying, 'Don't think I didn't see you.'

But that night, after a half-hearted attempt at repentance, I prayed the first honest prayer of my life. I am not sorry at all, I informed God. And as far as sex is concerned, I can't get rid of it, so if you want me to change, you'll have to do it for me. And then for a while, I knew the peace of God which passes understanding. An amused acceptance enveloped me, a kindness. Later, I learned to call it grace. And there have been many pomegranates since then, but few as sweet, many prayers but few as innocent, much grace but never so blissful.

This chapter was to have been written by John Turner. On Boxing Day 1996 John was walking along the pavement in Berlin on his way to take a Eucharist for a community of Franciscans when a car skidded on the ice and hit him. He died the next day. He was forty-two years old. This autobiographical fragment — the pomegranate story — is typical of John, full of humour and self-revelation. John's funeral in St George's, Berlin, and his memorial service in St Mary's Cathedral, Glasgow were both striking testimonies to his ministry. The churches were packed, full of people whose lives had been touched by this vulnerable man.

John's thinking, preaching and writing on sexuality was not by any means the whole story of the man, but it was an important part of him. I have tried to piece together some of his writing on sexuality and I hope I have done justice to my friend and colleague. He was a witty man with a great enthusiasm for people.

John's pastoral method was effective but unconventional. It consisted of long walks, cups of coffee, drinks in bars and convivial meals. Two friends in Berlin recite a familiar tale of how they got to know John — a quick cup of coffee after the morning service was still going strong in the wee small hours of the morning two meals and several bottles later. By then they were friends, I really mean 'friend', not the sort of acquaintance that passes for friendship but someone who knows the depth of your being.

An Australian friend, with antipodean subtlety, said of John: 'this screwed-up little man held all our lives together.' In conversations with friends John would reveal much about himself. He often said that we shouldn't hide our vulnerabilities, we should own them. John allowed his vulnerability to be obvious, part of his public self, and that allowed us to be open with him. Because he hid nothing about himself, his shortcomings, his sexuality, we didn't have to hide anything from him. Because he knew what it was to be screwed up, he knew the shape, the feel, the by-products of our screwed-upness. The empathy of a wounded healer is a precious thing. The huge congregations that filled two churches after his death testify to the rich harvest that daring to live in this vulnerable way can bring.

In Glasgow, in Berlin, his honesty about religion and about sex sometimes caused hostility among those who like tranquil certainties and a squeaky clean exterior. The mean-minded could and sometimes did attack him for what he was or what he said. But for most of us this quality made him such a valued counsellor and friend. A companion on the road, walking alongside amidst the hubbub of our lives.

This is not just hagiography but pertinent to the debate about sexuality. John's honesty and openness from the pulpit and in pastoral relationships helped to create a climate of honesty and integrity in which people can explore their sexuality. John would claim a gospel imperative for his inevitably non-judgemental stance. Jesus from Nazareth always welcomed people before they showed any hint of repentance or commitment. Liturgically John longed to be able to pronounce absolution before confession, thus removing the fear. Only when people feel welcomed and comfortable will there be any chance of a real meeting.

John quoted with approval Richard Holloway's remark that people are better at coping with the problems of dying than with the noisy problems of living.[1] We know what to do when confronted with a crisis or a death; we don't know what to do or say when confronted with the confusions and complexities of everyday life. The commendable rush of Christians to be trained as AIDS counsellors at the start of the pandemic is in sharp contrast to the lack of enthusiasm given to discussing issues of gay sexuality. John used to be exasperated that in Glasgow there were so many trained Christian AIDS counsellors ghoulishly waiting for people with HIV/AIDS, but still an unwillingness to acknowledge the five-ten per cent of gay people within their congregations.

The noisiest problem of all for Christians is sex. John was open about his sexuality and became a magnet for many people who wanted to talk about being gay. John's Gospel, his good news, included proclaiming 'the goodness of the body, the goodness of sexuality and of pleasure'. In a sermon which inevitably caused one or two members of the congregation to leave, but was also an example of why many more came to listen to John, he said:

> 'There is no room for fear in love,' says the introduction to the General confession. Fear; there I think we have the key to a great deal. For if there is no room for fear in love, it is equally sure and certain that there is precious little room for love where people are afraid. Fear of sex, of homosexuality, fear of difference and stigma, fear of suffering and death, fear of contact and intimacy. In the climate of fear, love does not flourish. Society engages in blame, in stereotyping, in denial, in scapegoating.[2]

This sermon, preached on World AIDS Day 1993, articulated some of the fear that the pandemic has brought; the subliminal messages conveyed by calling it a plague; the fear caused for young people now that sex and death are closely related thoughts; the fear of homosexual people — homophobia:

> Gay men and lesbians can arouse extraordinary reactions of fear, blame and envy. To be called a 'poof' or a 'dyke' in the school playground is about the worst insult of them all, and how many of us utterly outgrow the school playground in the course of our lives? I think the heart of the matter is fear, a fear that can cast out love. The heterosexual world feels uncomfortably challenged by the presence in its midst of women who don't really need men at all, thank you very much. And behind the need to deride and attack gay men is the fact of our fluid and sometimes ambivalent sexuality. To be an acceptable man in much of our society is still to be aggressive and heterosexual. So the gentle and homosexual elements in a young man's personality are often deeply suppressed and denied so that he can fit in with his mates. In an ordinary male environment with more or less of a premium on machismo, an overtly homosexual individual becomes both the object of scapegoating and furtive fascination. He is living out possibilities which his colleagues unconsciously fear and repress in themselves; he is a visible

reminder of what they are denied, and therefore must be shunned, at least in public. (It was, however, amusing to read in a recent Sunday supplement, of an 'out' gay policeman who, since emerging from the closet, had become the object of more discreet and optimistic advances from straight colleagues than he had ever dared hope for.)[3]

John had always been open to his bishops about his sexuality. He was exasperated by the church's attitude that seems to prefer furtive homosexual activity by a significant minority of its clergy rather than promoting stable gay relationships. The official pretence is that gay clergy are celibate. Everyone knows this to be false but because the assumption is there, it does nothing to take away the fear. John found church leaders pastorally kind and supportive but, with a few notable exceptions, unprepared to openly affirm gay clergy or stable gay relationships:

> There has been in many places much kindness and acceptance but not always the perfect love that casts out fear...Being loved is much nicer than just being tolerated.[4]

John had expressed that love and welcome to gay people through pastoral contact, through the struggle people have at edging open the closet door and through the blessing of gay couples. All of this he had done from clear gospel principles about inclusiveness. Had it been too much to hope that he and his fellow gay clergy would have received the same affirmation from the church? Of course gay clergy are tolerated, the church could not go on without them, but they are not allowed to be who they really are.

As a University Chaplain in Glasgow, only a minority of his students were gay, but his willingness to be open about his sexuality led many to talk about their own sexual fumblings and confusions. Honesty brings forth honesty. During a University mission, an evening question-and-answer session on 'Faith In Sexuality' raised for John a further example of the Christian community's inadequacy on matters sexual.

> The style was like *Any Questions?* but it was surprisingly eirenical. People listened respectfully to each other, and the contributions were universally frank and thoughtful. The spontaneous round of applause of the evening went to the young woman who articulated the feelings of the whole room. The churches, she declared, were failing her generation on the issues of sexuality. Conservative Christians presented a moral absolute which could be summed up as 'no sex outside marriage', but in today's world

few if any young people could or would adhere to that. Most people were like her, in the middle somewhere, not helped by the rigidities of the Christian Right, but not helped either by the liberal churches who tended to say nothing on the subject at all. Her generation felt itself to be facing complex moral issues without the help of a church. The applause was eloquent. I began to wonder about the silence of the liberals. Surely we were not quite silent, but did we commend or communicate principles as clearly as the conservatives with their rules and bible texts? What makes a good relationship? Can we walk lovingly with people while they explore that question? Are we afraid of the increasingly trackless jungle out there? Is it that we are in reaction against 'the law' ourselves and fear seeming to impose it, or fear of being accused of watering down Christian teaching to suit the self-indulgence of a Godless age?[5]

Since *Faith in the University* we often talked about how to break the silence. What to say to the young woman searching for a realistic sexual morality. John was attracted to the idea of 'emotional sincerity' of only saying and doing what you really mean, of the outer self expressing the inner self. Attractive as that is, and it shifts the debate to the quality of relationships rather than the rightness and the wrongness of sexual acts,[6] it is nevertheless a hard road to travel. Can we ever divine the inner self? Don't emotions cloud human reason? We talked about the idea of 'mutual consent' in which the guiding principle must be, 'Thou shalt not sexually manipulate, take advantage of, or abuse another person at any time.'[7] And that was the last serious conversation I had with John in a bar in Berlin.

John's Brethren background, with its narrow and exclusive attitudes made him a suitable person to lead people from a sexual morality based on fear to something more liberating. It was a journey he had painfully undertaken. His background helped him to understand the fundamentalism of many students and the repressed mess that this kind of theology can cause in people.

The Christian tide in Scotland is running in favour of conservative evangelicalism, even fundamentalism, these days, and if the mood of our Divinity faculties is anything to go by, it will not be long before that tendency is a sizeable majority in the Church of Scotland. But it will never be the only voice. Currently it is the loudest, and it addresses the fears and confusions of young people with an age-old temptation; exchange your scary, dangerous freedom for our set of rules. You'll know exactly where you are again. Right will be right and wrong will be wrong and that will be that.[8]

John in his small way helped to provide another voice. In his open and non-judgemental manner and by his honesty about his own vulnerabilities, he gave people the courage to open up and dare to leave the stranglehold of conservative evangelicalism. Through his attitude he was able to go some way to creating Christian communities that had moved from tolerance and acceptance of gay people to welcome and love of gay people. His aim was always to create communities where people could let the mask slip and be themselves without fear.

> God is love and we are his children.
> There is no room for fear in love.
> We love because he loved us first.[9]

Dreaming of Eden (iii)

Dreaming of Eden
I conjecture you
knowing everything

Tumbling towards a hard outcrop
we land together like homecoming
and are withstood

Dreaming my mouth on your face
yours on the veins of my wrist
all our exiles return

Dreaming innocence
knowing everything
we are cursed
we cannot fall

The happy fault: beyond innocence

I am a woman of my time, and my time is democratic. I live in a country, and in an era, where democracy is the prevailing political idea, and for this I am profoundly grateful. Though it is an idea which is often found wanting in practice, and though it is not the experience of many parts of the world, it is one which, thousands of years after its birth, has worked its way into human consciousness enough to become both an aspiration and an ideal for most of the globe. It is enshrined in legislation, in UN charters and declarations of human rights at every level.

So, even where it is absent in practice, the notion of human rights, of the equality of all persons of every gender, race, class and status, of their dignity and personhood, is shaping our individual consciousness and our world view. One of the fundamental consequences of democracy is that it gives to every person the right to be the subject of their own lives — to own their lives, if you like. And the corollary of that right of individuals is that it be the same for every other individual. We have the *right* to be subject up to and until it interferes with that right for others. Our *responsibility* in a democracy is to safeguard that right as much for others as we do for ourselves. The two are one and the same.

So, I am not territory, neither is my body, my mind, my soul, my sexuality, because I am one, autonomous. No-one can have territorial rights over me because of my gender, my ethnicity, my status.

And yet, to say this is to recognize a huge shift in human consciousness. In our sexuality, it is a liberation which has taken place for most women only over the last hundred years or so, and of course, unevenly. Nevertheless, it is an idea which will not be undone.

But to recognize and accept and affirm women as autonomous sexual persons is also a huge shift for men. And for neither women nor men is it an easy one.

Being conscious

It is not made any easier by being burdened by a church theology in which one or other or both parties in an exchange, a relationship, are deemed to be intrinsically bad, a theology in which their nature, rather than the nature of their exchange, is seen to be the locus of sin. In other words, it is *who we are* rather than *what we do* that is inherently evil. This theology of total depravity is, of course, one of the most hotly debated issues of doctrine in the whole of Christianity. In Pauline terms, it is the consequence of the Fall, directly attributable to the sin of Adam and Eve in the Garden, who ate of the fruit of the tree of knowledge of good and evil. By so doing, they became self-conscious. They knew their nakedness. This knowledge, to the mind of Paul, was the prerogative of God, and by laying claim to it, human beings trespassed on the divine territory.

There are probably few of us who have not lamented our self-consciousness at one time or another. How wonderful to be completely spontaneous, uninhibited, shameless. How wonderful not to observe ourselves, judge ourselves, convict ourselves. How wonderful to be unaffected by anything except the demands of the present moment, to be unaware of consequences. No wonder the desire to get back to the Garden is such a potent human myth. No wonder we take such delight in the innocence of small children, seeing in them as we do the time before the Fall.

And how sexually wonderful to be all of these things!

For there are probably few of us who have not also, like Paul, lamented the reality that we do inhabit, and which he describes so vividly: 'for, even though the desire to do good is in me, I am not able to do it. I don't do the good I want to do; instead, I do the evil that I do not want to do.' *(Romans 7:18-19)*

Two thousand years ago, Paul struggled heroically to construct a meaningful framework to explain the existence and persistence of human wrongdoing, and to show how Jesus offered a way beyond its dreary inevitability. And indeed, few have charted the *experience* of sin more profoundly. His way of addressing it, of interpreting its *causes*, was to split the human person into two parts.

Paul's struggle, owing much as it did to the Greek mind/body dualism of his time, is a profound and insightful description of the *feelings*, the inner experience of conflicting desires and values, not least of his own feelings. But that struggle has actually resulted in what he himself describes: 'I don't do the good I want to do; instead I do the evil that I don't want to do.' *(Romans 7:19)*

There can be few doctrines that have been so damaging to so many, can have so defaced the image of God as one which splits the human person into parts and declares the physical intrinsically bad. Still today, lovers and counsellors, therapists and doctors are helping to pick up the pieces of lives blighted by this interpretation. It has allowed all that is sensory and feeling, all that is instinctive and intuitive to be despised, and the intellectual and 'spiritual' to be idolized. It has deprived countless men and women and children of the experience of much of what is most delightful, most hopeful and most joyful about being human. It has divided people against themselves, against each other, and against God.

In a dangerous consequence of such a doctrine, it has allowed people to dissociate from their behaviour, refuse to assume responsibility for it, attribute it to the imperatives of their sinful 'human nature'. Paul says it himself: 'If I do what I don't want to do, this means that I am no longer the one who does it; instead, it is the sin that lives in me' *(Romans 7:20)*. This is the shadow side of 'an angel told me to do it'.

It is the ideology behind, 'I couldn't help myself' or 'it's human nature to fight wars' or 'all men are rapists'.

In a sense, it is the scapegoating of a part of ourselves, in order to blame, control or otherwise avoid assuming responsibility for our actions. We don't just do it to others, we have done it to ourselves. Or, one might say, Paul, and from him, the Christian church, has enabled that process. And it has the terrible effect of taking away the emphasis from where it should be; which is on the nature of the exchange, the transaction. I find this to be deeply unChristlike.

For Jesus, the exchange was all important, for it was in the exchange that the divine nature of right relationship was demonstrated. It is my understanding of Jesus, but more than that, it is my faith in him that all situations contain the possibility of redemption through the transformation of relationship. And that all people have the potential for salvation, for liberation, by being released from self-hatred and other-hatred not by the denial of the body but by its hallowing.

My dirty womb

Recently, I had the salutary experience of being in church where a version of the 'Liturgy of St James' was sung which included the phrase, 'Mary's spotless womb'. I lost the hymn after that — I was too busy thinking through the implications of the phrase. If

Mary's womb was spotless, did that mean that mine was spotted, stained, dirty even? And was it dirty because of what had come out of it, or what had been introduced into it? Were the children that had come out of it dirty, or the penis that had gone into it? Were the sexual acts that had resulted in the birth of the children dirty, or the giving birth to them out of it? And what about the sexual acts that hadn't resulted in pregnancy? Were they dirty? Or perhaps it was my very womb itself that was intrinsically dirty, because I had come from one like it? And what did 'dirty' mean, in this context? Did it simply mean dusty or earthy as one's hands might be after gardening, or was it a word loaded with metaphorical content of corruption and decay?

I asked these questions, and I thought of my beautiful children. I thought of the considerable pleasure, and occasional moments of ecstasy I have received, and I hope given, in making love. I thought of my forty-four-year-old body, bearing the marks of time, childbirth and breastfeeding, years of carrying shopping, of occasional illness or injury — the marks of mortality. As this body, I have worked, fed people, comforted children and adults, experienced the beauty and the tragedy of the world, sung, danced, wept, felt anger and tenderness, experienced pain and weakness, got around more reliably than with any form of mechanized transport ... the list is endless.

I was so angry, I nearly walked out of the service. Here is the legacy of the church, still subtly underpinning so much of our understanding of sexuality. Why are we still singing this pernicious garbage? It is not our *bodies* that are in need of redemption, it is our *consciousness*.

I *love* my body. I love the fact that I am a carnal, sexual being. I am thankful to God with every breath I take for my incarnation, and for the incarnation of Jesus that said a great *'yes'* to mine. I hate the things that damage people's bodies (and indeed, the bodies of animals, and of the earth itself) as much as I hate the things that damage the human spirit, because they cannot be divided. We are unitary beings, whole people. It is a false consciousness that has made one part of our human experience bad and one part good. This is the Christian legacy that we are only now beginning to shake off.

Because I do not feel my body, or anyone else's, for that matter, to be bad, and because dirt for me is a neutral word, to do with dishes or houses that need washed (and indeed, is sometimes a good word with associations of sweat after energetic activity or earth in a garden) the religious language of purity and impurity to describe sin is meaningless for me. Taboos around menstruation and childbirth, around bodily fluids and natural functions, which may have had their origins in ancient hygiene precautions but were extrapolated into cultural attitudes and practices, especially with regard to women, are not part of my consciousness. That this language still exerts a powerful emotional influence, is for me an indication that this is a part of the legacy we need to work hard at shaking off. There are many ways to describe the reality of sin; it may be separation, alienation, wrong relationship, but the language of impurity has blighted too many lives already.

Another part of that damaging legacy is a deep fear and distrust of pleasure, not only sexual pleasure, but especially that. And if pleasure comes in ways that are not sanctioned, are outwith the control of those with power, then it is particularly threatening. Nothing challenges authority more strongly than pleasure, nothing is more subversive of a status quo than the idea that people might be having a better time outside it. Then it is necessary to minimize its appeal, to put awful penalties on it, to make it so dangerous that people will be thoroughly frightened off. Then control can be regained. One could make a good case for the homophobic injustice often found in the church having its roots in sheer fury at the fact that gay culture is open about its enjoyment of sex.

The need to minimize and penalize and police sexual pleasure can lead church pronouncements to display a naïveté that exposes them to the potential for ridicule, or sheer incomprehension on the part of their hearers. There is a religious syndrome which might be termed 'the raging inferno' syndrome, which regards human sexuality as a fire which, unless it is safely contained and controlled within the domestic grate of marriage, will inevitably and immediately turn into a fireball of rape, incest and paedophilia, with no other or intermediate possibilities. Or the one which genuinely believes that only sex within marriage can be fulfilling, loving, tender and safe, responsible and creative. Both these positions simply do not reflect the breadth and depth of human experience.

None of this is to say that sex in every circumstance is good, or that pleasure is necessarily an end in itself. This is patently not so. But it is to suggest that the consciousness with which many, perhaps most people in our society view sexuality, their sexual world view, is not based on the same premises that traditional Christian teaching about sexuality is based on. It is a different consciousness.

A different way of knowing

Traditional Christian doctrine on sexuality is based on patriarchy, on the body as corrupt (especially the bodies of women), and of sensory and sexual pleasure as suspect. Contemporary consciousness is democratic, affirming of the physical, and understands pleasure as a good thing.

Furthermore, there is conflict between a Christian view which holds human nature and biology to be fixed and unchanging, and a contemporary understanding of these as dynamic, fluid, and, over aeons, continually evolving. And in a pluralistic society, we are made ever more aware of different understandings of human sexuality, relationship and practice, different ways of being family and community, many of which seem to contribute as much, if not more, to human wellbeing. Jews, Buddhists, Muslims, Hindus, humanists, atheists, agnostics all know about love, about fidelity, about the sacrificial nature of parenting, about the agony and ecstasy, and the mundanity and frustration of sexual relationship of every kind. Christians are not the only people who know about love, and the evidence to suggest that what we have to say about it is any better, more enlightened or more nurturing of human community is somewhat limited.

Indeed, there is a certain irony in the fact that when Christian moralists lament and lambast 'me first' individualism as being the cause of everything from the breakdown of the nuclear family to lack of respect for authority, they are simply seeing replicated on an individual scale (in this age of democracy) what was most effectively practised by British imperialism a century ago against other countries, abrogating to itself the right to have what it wanted, when it wanted, no matter the cost to others. Such imperialism, of course, was sanctioned by the church, whose golden age of mission it was!

Human rights for women, the availability of contraception, the education and thence the economic independence of women, have led to the democratization of the relationship between the sexes. For perhaps the first time in human history, there is the possibility, the idea, of women as autonomous, free and equal human beings in everything including their sexuality.

But as all countries who move from being dependent to independent experience, this is a terribly hard transition to make; and not only for them, but for those who previously ruled them.

For women, these are the challenges of freedom and autonomy. Recently, the National Household Survey was published in Britain which suggested that forty per cent of all single women aged between sixteen and forty-nine were at any one time not active sexually; that is, they were not in relationships, or not looking for relationships, or had chosen to be celibate. This phenomenon — all these women who could be having sex and weren't! — evoked a flurry of media musings, many from feminist commentators. Suzanne Moore, writing in *The Independent*, ventured the thought that perhaps we have just had enough, that we have become such a sexually saturated culture that we have reached the point of over-consumption. Now women are becoming more discriminating.

> I suspect the abstainers may know what makes them happy. Or they may simply view sex as being about more than physical need. Women, accustomed to increased choices in every area of their lives, are making choices in this department too. Contraception has freed us up, work has given us independence. Many women view sex as part of the deal, not as the deal itself. They want partners to fit in with a lifestyle they have prepared earlier, instead of changing their lives around when they meet a man.[1]

Shane Watson, in *The Guardian*, sees it somewhat differently. In her view, it's all about control:

> Get dressed up, look good, go to the party and flirt by all means, but can you really afford to take it all off and let go? ... you must deliberately adopt an attitude that couldn't possibly be mistaken for desperation, so you end up behaving like a supermodel at a soiree. You won't meet the eye of anyone single in case they should get the impression you are on the pull. Multiply this faux disinterest by two for the single men, and you've got a no-contact situation ... now you've both got to anticipate a vigorous power struggle in the first 24 hours.[2]

Joyce MacMillan, in a piece entitled, 'No sex please — we're all brutish Puritans' in *Scotland on Sunday* sees it as more deep-rooted:

> At heart ... we are still a joyless bunch of Puritans, a million miles from that big, splashy passion for life that would enable us to take pleasure in all of its processes, instead of shuddering away from them with a fear and distaste that took generations to educate into us, and will no doubt take centuries to educate out.[3]

All these perspectives share one thing; the assumption that the sexual activity, or lack of it, of single women, is a matter of personal choice. This is a huge change from the times within living memory, when the assumption was that *no* single woman should be sexually active, and that if she was then she was no better than she should be.

Of course there are many women in this society who don't assume that kind of freedom, who are not economically independent, for whom that kind of choice is perceived as a burden rather than a gift. But the choices and responsibilities of autonomy and freedom are an ideal and an aspiration for many who don't now enjoy them — and for girls growing up. And these choices and responsibilities include choices about what constitutes right relationships.

If Suzanne Moore is right, and what we are seeing now is the passing of the first splurge of freedom, in which 'we do because we can' is followed by 'we don't because we can too'(or at least, we are more discriminating about when and with whom we do), and because being 'a good shag' or 'a great wee ride' seems a rather reduced kind of human exchange, then the withdrawal of women into their own space is a logical next stage. Perhaps it goes with the wisdom gained by listening to the body and its instinctive knowledge about our appetites and what really satisfies; which is rarely junk food, however enjoyable it may be once in a great while.

And having so lately gained autonomy, the desire not to lose control, to be once again vulnerable, is very understandable. It is a huge risk to take, and for a great many women, confidence in men to be safe, to be respectful and to be reciprocal is quite limited. The free-market pressures to be successful, strong and in which presentation rather than substance is all-important, (as demanding and difficult for men as for women) simply exacerbate the danger of vulnerability and risk-taking. Men and women are guarded with each other, unsure of the new ground between them.

Are we therefore looking at the kind of relationships characterized thus by the poet Rainer Maria Rilke: 'Love consists in this; that two solitudes border and protect and salute each other.'[4]? There is no doubt that for many, this is a preferable option to what the possibilities were in the past. But it's not exactly Joyce MacMillan's 'big, splashy passion for life'. If passion for life requires anything, it is the ability to not mind making a fool of oneself, the ability to be spontaneous.

And so we are back at the Garden. Or at least, we are at its gate. For most of us, there is, in fact, no going back. We will not trade our consciousness for innocence. The price of the myth was too high. But is there another way onward from Eden that is not about subjection and corruption and suffering? When we stand outside the myth, is there anything left in Christianity that is different, that is worth saving and saying, worth bearing witness to in human sexuality.

The nature of the exchange

> You hung there
> brown eyed
> blood dripping
> from the thorns
> digging into your head.
>
> I was taught
> to imagine
> how you suffered
> and I was told
> you suffered for me.
>
> I couldn't grasp
> what that meant.
> If you suffered
> for me
> why did I suffer too?[5]

A lot of people have asked that question? But what if we were to read Christ from a different starting point? If we believe that Jesus reveals God to us, and God in relation to humankind, then what I see is not a petulant, prohibitive God, but a divine permissiveness which desires nothing more than our wellbeing, whose pleasure it is to give us the kingdom (or perhaps even the Garden). In this reading, there is an invitation to right relationship, to something fuller, freer and more satisfying than we have previously known.

One of the losses of our present guardedness is that the nature and extent of our relationships can very easily become terribly reduced, leaving us too often with only the sexual relationship, the nuclear family, and the single person, bearing the weight of all our human needs and desires — and all of these cracking under that burden. This is an emotionally emaciated condition.

For Jesus, there was no such thing as the single person. There was only the community, and those who, for some reason, had been excluded or isolated from the community — foreigners, outcasts of every kind, destitute and homeless people, those in mental distress, 'harlots'. These he brought back into relationship within the community, in a series of exchanges which transformed people's consciousness about themselves, about others, and about God. Exclusion against one's will was wrong relationship for Jesus.

Though these exchanges were different, some joyful, some sorrowful, all of them seem to me to share certain characteristics. Firstly, every one of them is marked by a generosity of heart and spirit, by going beyond where legality requires them to go. Secondly, they are spontaneous, they leap out in a self-forgetful way, whether in gladness or compassion or care. Thirdly, that spontaneity is drawn out by some deep respect for, or delight in the otherness of the other, in who they are. Fourthly, the exchange is one of freedom — there is no coercion in the response, whether through fear or law or the desire for approval. And finally, something changes for the better because of the exchange. All, whether giver or receiver, gain. And the integration of the excluded one into an extended and wider community, back into relationship, is the context of the exchange. The exchange is redemptive. For Jesus, part of the consequence of love, of the outrageous and subversive transformation of relationship, was indeed suffering. It may be a consequence for us. That is no reason to idealize and idolize suffering. Why should we desire anyone to suffer for us? To love us — that is a different thing.

The community that Jesus created was one of free and autonomous co-equals; 'not servants but friends' *(John 15:15)*. In our autonomous and mobile society of individuals, in which traditional communities based on geography, work, class or religion are increasingly breaking down, perhaps attention to the structures, values and practices that affirm and rebuild inclusive, just and compassionate communities would bring us into a more diverse experience of relationship and a more natural context for relaxing and taking a few risks. Perhaps we need to discover new ways of being *human* together in order to find the new ways of being men and women, or women and women, or men and men together. Perhaps there is a reweaving needed of the web of life that itself supports us through the times when we betray and hurt one another, as we inevitably do.

Our deepest hungers — for acceptance, for affirmation of our lovability and our value regardless of achievement — may find nourishment in one lifelong partner. They may find nourishment in a community of relationships. They may find nourishment in celibacy, or even in great solitude, in commitment to justice-making or in creative work. People are different, and should be allowed to remain so. And yet there is that in us which remains unfilled and unfulfilled, even in the best relationship or the happiest family. Religious people have described this as the yearning for God, others as the longing for connection with all that is, with the ground of our being. Perhaps it is the desire for our truest and deepest selves, the self which wants to be whole, to come home, the self to which we are over and over again unfaithful.

This completion I do not think we ever find in the Adam or Eve of the myth; 'you complete me' is the slogan of dangerous innocence. It so easily turns to 'meet my needs', and, 'I only exist to meet your needs'. Letting go of the burden of perfection, practising forgiveness, entering into the pattern of life and death and resurrection, of love and loss, letting go and renewal, these to me are the way of redemption, and its context is always exchange, with others, with ourselves, with God.

> The bodies of grownups
> come with stretchmarks and scars,
> faces that have been lived in,
> relaxed breasts and bellies,
> backs that give trouble,
> and well-worn feet:
> flesh that is particular,
> and obviously mortal.
> They also come with bruises on their heart,
> wounds they can't forget,
> and each of them
> a company of lovers in their soul
> who will not return
> and cannot be erased.
> And yet I think there is a flood of beauty
> beyond the smoothness of youth;
> and my heart aches for that grace of longing
> that flows through bodies
> no longer straining to be innocent,
> but yearning for redemption.[6]

The happy fault

I want to end by bearing witness. I am someone who has experienced marital breakdown and divorce. I got married very young, and when I look back now, I think I lived in a kind of innocence. Though not, I hope, unkind or uncaring, I lived with a kind of emotional security blanket, my own little Eden wrapped round me. I never had really to face what it was like to feel loneliness or rejection, fear or failure. Though not everything in my garden was rosy, I never questioned that I would always live there. So when the fall came, it was as if my world had crumbled, a driving-out from the garden. I was a good person, I thought, things like this were not supposed to happen to people like me. I was used to being strong, to helping people, to coping. Now I had to get used to asking others for help. I had to swallow a lot of pride.

I was also very angry — with other people, with myself, with God. But I wasn't prepared to ask for anything that wasn't given freely. Law seemed despicable if there was coercion in it. And for the last year of my marriage, I understood in a deep way what it means to live in sin, in which the rings on our fingers were a complete irrelevance. It means to be divided, far apart, alien, almost. This wrong relationship was not so much about what either of us had done or failed to do. In fact, we had both tried very hard. I think we did not, and have not, stopped loving each other in some way. But since we could each barely live with ourselves, we could not live with each other.

Then I read something written by Gerard Hughes in *God of Surprises*. It said, 'the facts are kind. God is in the facts'.[7] I was outraged! But I couldn't get it out of my mind. I started to look for God in the facts. This was a painful process. I had to address my own divisions, the places where I was not just the victim but the one causing the suffering. My anger was replaced by sorrow and shame. My consciousness was being changed. Paralysed outside the gate, seeing clearly for the first time some of the barrenness of my garden, I did not know which way to go. But then I found that God came to me as the ground beneath my feet, and I could start to walk again, away from the garden, without a clue where I was going.

The five years since then have not always been easy, and I've had some bad moments in the precarious wilderness outside the garden. But more and more, I think of them as grace. I have learned much more about what it means to live in trust, and to give thanks for my daily bread. I mean, bread that day. I have learned to see the beauty outside the garden, and there have been many people who have been for me the face of God. Some of them I would never have noticed in the garden. I have a community of relationships vivid in the colours they are painted with. I have learned to love my solitude.

My relationship with my children, who were my main anxiety and guilt, has become a well of living water. They too, innocent as they were, had to leave the garden. They were young to lose their innocence, and it hurt them. But they, more than anyone, have taught me the meaning of forgiveness and unconditional love. And now I am not too downcast about their lives, because I see that for them too, redemption is a possibility. Part of that redemptive possibility lies in the nature of the exchanges with and of their parents. To work at these, as all of us have done, has not been easy. But it has borne fruit. Now, for the first time in years, I think that my ex-husband (who has since remarried) and I are in right relationship. It is a different relationship, with much greater space between us. But in relation to our children, we are a free community of equals.

I discover that I prefer life outside the garden. I don't want to go back, I want to go forward. Although I have regret for what might have been, I don't have it for what is. My self-understanding is different now, including my sexual self-understanding and I am glad. It has left behind much traditional Christian doctrine. Maybe that means I am no longer a Christian. But I believe it is where following Jesus has taken me.

> We die containing a richness of lovers and tribes, tastes we have swallowed, bodies we have plunged into and swum up as if rivers of wisdom, characters we have climbed into as if trees, fears we have hidden as if in caves. I wish for all this to be marked on my body when I am dead. I believe in such cartography — to be marked by nature, not just to label ourselves on a map like the names of rich men and women on buildings. We are communal histories, communal books. We are not owned or monogamous in our taste or experience. All I desired was to walk upon such an earth that had no maps.[8]

There is an ancient part of the liturgy for Holy Saturday, the day before the Resurrection is celebrated on Easter Day, which refers to the Fall, and the sin of Adam and Eve which led to it, as the 'happy fault': 'O happy fault, which merited a redemption so great and of such a kind'.[9]

The facts are kind, and God is in the facts.

Bibliography

Scriptures quoted from the *Good News Bible* published by
The Bible Societies/HarperCollins Publishers Ltd UK ©
American Bible Society, 1966, 1971, 1976, 1992

Introduction; Kathy Galloway

1   Kathy Galloway, from 'Shame', *Talking To The Bones*,
SPCK, 1996

Coming home; Ruth Burgess

This poem was written for someone joining the church. It
was first published in *The Pattern of Our Days: Liturgies
and resources for worship*, edited by Kathy Galloway (Wild
Goose Publications, The Iona Community, Glasgow, 1996)
p. 131

Wild uncharted seas: sexuality and belonging; Anna Briggs

1   Thomas Cranmer, 'the confession in Morning Prayer and
Evening Prayer', *Book of Common Prayer 1662*, Church of
England

2   H. A. Williams, *Someday I'll Find You* (Mitchell Beazley
International, London, 1982. Fount Paperbacks, London,
1982) pp. 44-45

3   *Ibid.*, p. 239

4   *Ibid.*, p. 124

5   Anna Briggs, from her play about the life of Josephine
Butler, 'Not Counting The Women and Children'

6   H. A. Williams, *op.cit.*, p. 243

7   Dannie Abse, 'Epithalamion', *Collected Poems 1948-1976*
(Hutchinson & Co Ltd, London, 1977) pp. 2-3

Nighmares in the garden: Christianity and sexual violence; Lesley Macdonald

1 Statistics derived from various sources, including Zero Tolerance Campaign material; International Conference held in Brighton, November 1996: 'Violence, Abuse and Women's Citizenship'

2 Joni Mitchell, extract from 'Woodstock', appears on the album, *Ladies of the Canyon* (Siquomb Publishing Co, 1969 Reprise Records 1970)

3 John Milton, extract from *Paradise Lost* (1.297)

4 Augustine, *Literal Commentary on Genesis*, quoted in E. A. Clark, *Women in the Early Church*, Lewiston, New York: Edwin Mellen 1984) p. 29

5 This quotation is from a book entitled *Sexuality and Subordination,* written by Susan Mendus and Jane Rendell (Routledge, 1989)

6 Texts of terror — this refers to the title of Phillis Tribble's book, *Texts of Terror: Literary feminist readings of biblical narratives* (Fortress Press, Philadelphia, 1984)

7 This refers to a letter written by the Pope to Archbishop Vinko Puljic of Sarajevo, and a subsequent front page editorial in the Milan newspaper, *Corriere della Sera*: both were quoted in an article by Colette Douglas-Home (*The Scotsman,* 4 March 1993)

8 Karl Bartl, *Church Dogmatics*, Vol 3, part 4 (English translation published by T & T Clark, Edinburgh, p.172)

9 John Knox, 'First Blast of the Trumpet Against the Monstrous Regiment of Women', in M A Breslow, *The Political Writings of John Knox* (Washington: Folger Books, 1985) p. 43

10 Eva Lundgren, 'I Am Endowed with All the Power in Heaven and on Earth — When men become men through "Christian" abuse', in *Studia Theologica* 48 (1994) p.39

11 Marvin Ellison, 'Common decency: A New Christian Sexual Ethics', by J B Nelson and S P Longfellow, (editors) *Sexuality and the Sacred: Sources for Theological Reflection* (London: Mowbray 1994) p. 239

Man to (wo)man; Peter Anderson

This poem was first published in issue 3/28 of *Coracle,* the magazine of the Iona Community

Flame within my being: Incarnating feminist theology; Elizabeth South

1   Margaret Guenther, *Holy Listening* (DLT, London, 1992) p. 119
2   Daphne Hampson, *Theology and Feminism* (Basil Blackwell,Oxford 1990) p. 169

For the rest of your life: the reconstruction and deconstruction of marriage; John and Molly Harvey

1   *The Diary of A Young Girl: Anne Frank: The definitive version* (translated by Otto H Frank and Miriam Pressler, Viking, 1996), p. 200

Celibacy: a subversive proclamation of Christian freedom, or sexual repression; Mary Shanahan

Sources   *The Way* Supplement, 1993/77 Celibacy
Sally Cline, *Women,Celibacy and Passion* (Andre Deutsch, 1993)

The cost of denial; John Turner

This chapter, written by the late John Turner, was first published by St Mary's Cathedral, Glasgow, 1993

1   Dom Helder Camara, from a Christian Aid poster
2   Kenneth Leech, from *Care and Conflict: Leaves from a pastoral notebook* (DLT, London, 1990) p. 17
3   Rowan Williams, from *Speaking Love's Name* (Jubilee Group pamphlet, 1988) page 1 of introduction

No fear in love; John Turner and Peter Francis

1   Richard Holloway, Anger, Sex, Doubt and Death (SPCK, London, 1992)
2   John Turner, World AIDS Day Sermon, St Mary's Cathedral, Glasgow 1993
3   John Turner, *Ibid.*
4   John Turner, *Ibid.*
5   John Turner, 'Faith In The University', in The Avenue, Glasgow University, 1994
6   John Macmurray, 'The Virtue of Chastity', in *Reason and Emotion* (Faber & Faber 1935)
7   Anne Borrowdale, *Distorted Images* (SPCK, 1991) p. 127 quoting Marie Fortune
8   John Turner, 'Faith In The University', *op.cit.*
9   Invitation to Confession in Scottish Episcopal Church Liturgy 1982 (based on 1 John 4:16-19)

The happy fault: beyond innocence; Kathy Galloway

1   Suzanne Moore, extract from 'Phoning in sick from the sexual revolution' (*The Independent*, 21March 1997)

2   Shane Watson, extract from 'No sex, please, we're single' (*The Guardian*, 20 March 1997)

3   Joyce MacMillan, extract from 'No sex, please — we're all brutish Puritans' (*Scotland on Sunday*, 23 March 1997)

4   Rainer Maria Rilke, *Letters to a Young Poet* (Langley & Sons, London, 1943); (Sidgwick & Jackson, London, 1945)

5   Kay Carmichael, 'The Suffering Christ' in *Sweet, sour and serious* (Survivors' Press, Scotland, 1996) p. 123

6   Janet Morley, *All Desires Known* (SPCK, London, 1992)

7   Gerard Hughes, *God of Surprises* (DLT, London, 1985); this phrase appears throughout the book

8   Michael Ondaatje, *The English Patient* (Bloomsbury, London, 1992) p. 261

9   'The happy fault', from the *Book of Common Prayer*, 1552

The Iona Community

The Iona Community is an ecumenical Christian community, founded in 1938 by the late Lord MacLeod of Fuinary (the Rev. George MacLeod DD) and committed to seeking new ways of living the Gospel in today's world. Gathered around the rebuilding of the ancient monastic buildings of Iona Abbey, but with its original inspiration in the poorest areas of Glasgow during the Depression, the Community has sought ever since the 'rebuilding of the common life', bringing together work and worship, prayer and politics, the sacred and the secular in ways that reflect its strongly incarnational theology.

The Community today is a movement of some 200 Members, over 1,400 Associate Members and about 1,600 Friends. The Members — women and men from many backgrounds and denominations, most in Britain, but some overseas — are committed to a rule of daily prayer and Bible reading, sharing and accounting for their use of time and money, regular meeting and action for justice and peace.

The Iona Community maintains three centres on Iona and Mull: Iona Abbey and the MacLeod Centre on Iona, and Camas Adventure Camp on the Ross of Mull. Its base is in Community House, Glasgow, where it also supports work with young people, the Wild Goose Resource and Worship Groups, a bimonthly magazine (*Coracle*) and a publishing house (Wild Goose Publications).

For further information on the Iona Community please contact:

The Iona Community,
Pearce Institute,
840 Govan Road,
Glasgow
G51 3UU

T. 0141 445 4561; F. 0141 445 4295
email: ionacomm@gla.iona.org.uk
http://www.iona.org.uk